UNSINKABLE

*Sunk by a freighter on their way to paradise,
a cruising couple's strength and perseverance
help rebuild their life and dreams*

Dee Saunders

FINE EDGE
Nautical & Recreational Publishing

Cover and Book Design by Melanie Haage
Edited by Leslie Bunzel
Copyedited by Linda Scantlebury and Polly Lane
Back cover photos by the author and Mark Bunzel
All other photos by the author except where noted

First Edition.
Printed in the United States.
10 9 8 7 6 5 4 3 2 1

Library of Congress Cataloging in Publication Data is available.

Fine Edge
Nautical and Recreational Publishing
14004 Biz Point Lane, Anacortes, WA 98221
tel 360-299-8500
fax 360-299-0535
www.FineEdge.com

DEDICATION

I dedicate this book to all of our family and friends who helped in so many ways in our rapid return to both our home and our way of life; and to my mother who instilled in me the belief that nothing was impossible to do, if I wanted to do it. I can still hear her sing her little song, "I can do it; I can do it, if I try." I had no idea that those little words would carry me through my entire life. To this day I never understand why people give up on their dreams, their goals, their lives. I guess they never had a mother who sang that song or had someone repeat those words to them hundreds of times. Thank you, mother, for giving me the confidence to know that "I can do it, if I try."

TABLE OF CONTENTS

ACKNOWLEDGMENT

I would like to thank Kathy for giving me direction, Sidonia for constantly reminding me "I can do it," my husband Marshall for his patience, and most of all to my sister, Lynn, who helped me relive our life's adventures and tragedies and finally verbalize them in a way that I could share them with all of you.

Prologue

MARSHALL AND I ARE OPPOSITES—PROBABLY AS OPPOSITE as two people can be and still find common ground on which to base a relationship.

Marshall is up with the sun and ready to *do something*—ready to do anything, including finding innovative new ways to wake me up. I like to stay nestled under the warm covers for hours, reading.

Marshall likes chaos and clutter and leaves a continuous trail any woman could follow and know exactly where he had been and what his every activity and movement had been that day. I like calm and organization: A place for everything and for everything to stay in its place. I guess one could say I am a neatnik bordering on the side of anal. Clutter causes confusion in my thinking to the point that I can't start cooking a new meal until everything—and I mean *everything*—is put away in the kitchen and there is a clean, uncluttered work area for me to start anew.

I am slow and methodical when I take on projects. Marshall is fast and unpredictable. We are the perfect tortoise-and-hare example. During our real-estate era, we built a few speculative homes on which we did a lot of the work ourselves, including clearing the lots. Marshall would attack trees with a dynamic vigor, using his trusty chain saw. After a few hours he would collapse on a log, exhausted. I moved at a snail's pace picking up branches, putting them on burn piles and raking the area to give a manicured appearance. I could go on for hours at my pace. The point is, it took us in opposite approaches to complete a project and do a good job.

During our cruising days in Mexico we spent a lot of time snorkeling. The most enjoyable part for me was to float silently above a reef and observe the incredible interaction of the fish. I could stay in one spot and watch them for hours. Marshall liked to snorkel to "kill" something.

We also both loved to explore. It was almost a daily routine that Marshall would entice me to join him for a dinghy ride.

"I'll go warm up the engine," he would yell as he started down the ladder. "How soon can you be ready?"

"Give me five minutes and I'll be there. Just let me grab a few things," I would answer as I raced around gathering everything I thought necessary for the excursion.

Of course, we needed life jackets, the first aid kit, portable VHF radio, windbreakers, the flare kit, and anything else in sight I thought might be useful if we had a problem. I would just about get all the things handed down to Marshall and have one foot in the dinghy before he would have the throttle pushed forward, ready to speed away. Off he would fly, looking for the highest wave to jump. With my hair already plastered to the side of my head from the speed and wind, I would grab the lifelines and hang on for dear life.

Over the roar of the engine and in between trying to keep from being thrown out of the boat, I would yell, "I thought we were going to explore the coastline."

My idea of exploring was to slowly putt along the shore with my head hung over the side of the dinghy searching for wildlife and interesting sea life along the way, not flying by the coast at Mach One.

The only response I would get from Marshall was, "I can't hear what you are saying," and a "Yahoo!" as we flew over another wave.

Half an hour later Marshall would be headed full throttle toward the beach. He would time the waves, and then, just like surfing, he would pick up on a perfect one and ride it all the way to shore—throttle wide open, of course. We had done this many times, so I had learned to prepare for the landing. I would kneel on the floor and as we approached the beach lower my head over my knees and cling to the lines on the side of the dinghy. We would land with such force that if I or anyone else was still sitting on the side of the dinghy, there was a good chance we would be thrown out and onto the sand.

After coming to a screeching halt on the beach, I would raise my head slowly, checking to see if I was still all in one piece. Then I would turn to look at Marshall, only to see a huge grin plastered across his face.

He would chuckle and then, trying to humor me would ask enthusiastically, "Now wasn't that fun? Ready to go explore the town?"

I would sigh and rearrange my clothes and hair as I pulled myself out of the dinghy. Any semblance of neatness I had fastidiously tried to bestow upon myself before leaving on our dinghy exploration was long gone. My groomed hair was soaked and plastered to my head, my clothes were wrinkled and wet, and the adrenaline rush we had just experienced left me feeling as though we had just run the Indianapolis 500.

"You want to explore the town?" I would dubiously ask. I was familiar with Marshall's idea of exploring.

When arriving at a new area, part of the adventure and fun was to stroll around the village. I would love poking my head into the quaint shops, visiting the ornately decorated churches and relaxing at the central parks. There was always a tall hill beckoning me to take the perfect picture of our boat *Penguin* bobbing at anchor in the middle of the harbor.

But I knew from past experience that Marshall's idea of exploring the town and taking in local color was totally opposite mine. He enjoyed sitting in the local bar at the *bottom* of the hill having nachos and beer and watching locals do the walking as they passed by.

One of Marshall's many strong qualities is his incredible ability to stay calm in an emergency. He is able to assess a situation and react in rote fashion with accurate decisions. He is my knight in shining armor, and it is because of this quality that Joe, our crewmember aboard *Clambake*, and I are alive today.

On the other hand, I am useless in an emergency. I freeze and focus on little things, such as if my shoelaces are tied or if my socks match.

My strengths blossom when the crisis is over. I'm strong, positive, patient, and optimistic about the future. That is when Marshall relies on me.

I can't tell you how many times Marshall has asked, "Do you really think that is possible?"

I'm very patient and able to visualize the fruition of plans extending over several years. The "P" word, as we refer to the word *patient*, does not exist in Marshall's vocabulary. A long time to him is 37seconds. Keeping him in a positive state of mind after a crisis or after we have decided on a goal is a daily ordeal. At such times he reminds me of a caged cat, pacing back and forth and feeling trapped in a time warp.

Although we are opposites in so many ways, we enjoy doing the same things. We complement each other in work, in play, and in social situations, and are fortunate to possess qualities that fill gaping voids in each other's personality.

In addition, we both are very competitive and share a firm commitment to our goals. One could say we always have been *more* than committed to our goals: We have been passionate in our desire to achieve them and our aspiration to succeed has been as strong and as consistent as the moon's daily pull on the tides.

It is through our opposite attributes that we were, and still are, able to accomplish what would have been impossible for either of us on his or her own. For years we had planned an early retirement and to cruise the world in our own boat. Despite obstacles fate put in our path, working together we ultimately were able to achieve our dream in a way neither Marshall nor I could have ever imagined, proving what my mother had preached for years: "If you have a dream and the desire, you can do it if you try."

CHAPTER 1

Night of Terror Revisited

THE SEAS WERE CALM, THE SWELL LAPPED PLACIDLY AT OUR ship's huge steel hull as we glided smoothly through the water on our way to the South Pacific. The skies were cloudless and a gentle wind barely kissed my cheek. Our new boat, *Penguin*, was nestled among the megayachts and sat securely in her cradle welded to the steel deck of the 700-foot super transport. We were riding piggyback on a freighter this trip.

There was no land in sight. Everything was going on schedule. Yet, as I stood on the bow and stared at the horizon, I felt an uneasiness creep over me; my heart started to beat faster.

My mind drifted back to that day five years earlier when we had left the same Mexican coast on our own sailboat. How excited we were to begin the journey we had set as our goal for so many years.

Suddenly, a chill ran down my spine and fear gripped me as I recalled that dreadful night. The memories returned as vividly as if the events were happening all over again.

That March 15th also had been warm, with a cloudless sky; the wind was perfect at 12 to 15 knots. We had just raised the sails and watched our dependable *Clambake*, a 52-foot Tayana sloop, do what she did best, move fast with the wind. We had untied the dock lines and been ushered out of the harbor at Puerto Vallarta to shouts of "safe sailing," wishes for smooth seas and gentle breezes, and all the blessings bestowed upon sailors planning to spend a lot of time in Neptune's territory.

Marshall had chosen a spot about 10 degrees north of the Equator and set a compass course of about 220 degrees. We were hoping ultimately to shoot for a spot about four degrees north of the Equator and at about 124 degrees west longitude. We had 3,000-plus miles of ocean to cross, and wanted to begin our journey on a comfortable angle of sail by taking advantage of the northeast trades as long as possible before turning south and going through the doldrums and across the Equator.

We knew that if we left too early in March we would risk running into a hurricane in the South Pacific. On the other hand, if we dove through the doldrums too early or too far to the east, we might encounter southeast trades not yet fully formed. Such winds could be fluky instead of consistent, and delay our crossing. Marshall had been through the doldrums twice before; the first time it took only eight hours, but the second time he had to motor for four and a half days until he made it through. Ultimately, we would need to vary our course as the winds shifted, but for now we were enjoying a beautiful sail on a beam reach, traveling a comfortable seven knots.

Although this was my first ocean crossing, I felt no apprehension. Marshall was a seasoned sailor and his endless knowledge and talents made me feel totally at ease with the voyage. I knew he was capable of handling any situation or emergency that might arise. Also, I had confidence in *Clambake*; she was a well-maintained performance sailing vessel, and she was behaving flawlessly. Everything was going perfectly. We felt confident this was an omen for an easy crossing, and optimistic that our projected three-week schedule wouldn't be hard to maintain.

The first hour out, we set up a watch schedule. We had agreed to four-hour watches to begin at 1800. We also agreed it would be important to adhere to a schedule, but not the first night. The adrenaline was flowing and early to bed didn't feel right. So we talked about the future and about how we would handle bad weather (that old nemesis is never far from a sailor's thoughts) or a medical emergency. But most of all we talked about how we expected to enjoy months of sailing in Tahiti as our reward.

Marshall and I forced ourselves to go below to sleep about 2200. He had turned on the running lights and rechecked our course before joining me below. We were sailing on a straight 220-degree course. The winds were still a steady 12 to 15 knots and the sky crystal clear.

Because visibility was perfect, we decided to conserve our batteries by turning off the radar. As long as conditions stayed the same, we shouldn't have to make any course changes, we reasoned.

As a precaution, Marshall decided to sleep in the main salon that first night at sea. He wanted to be close enough to hear Joe—a good sailing friend whom we had asked to join us for the crossing—in case he needed any help on his first night's watch.

I climbed into our aft bunk and quickly drifted into a deep sleep.

Just before 0100 we were jarred awake by an incredible thud. I felt myself being thrown up against the sidewall of my cabin. It was as if our boat had hit a concrete wall in the middle of the ocean.

"Oh my God, Marshall, what did we hit? What's happening?" I screamed.

"I don't know," he yelled back.

Marshall had been thrown onto the floor in the main salon, but already had scrambled onto his feet and was headed for the companionway. I could hear him muttering as he started to scramble up the stairs, "OK, that didn't sound too bad. We can survive whatever that was."

My memory of the initial impact was totally different than Marshall's. I could hear the crushing and shattering of fiberglass and the incomprehensible sounds of our boat breaking apart. I felt huge beams with jagged edges stabbing me fiercely on the side of my head. I remember putting my hand to the side of my face and feeling something sticky running down my cheek.

Lying there for a second, I tried to grasp what was happening outside. *It had to be a nightmare—a really terrible nightmare.*

As I gathered my wits and tried to crawl out of my bunk, there was another horrendous crash. I was thrown unbelievably hard against the wall a second time. This impact was a lot more gut wrenching than the first; it sounded and felt like a wrecking ball meeting a brick building. An intense screeching sound of metal scraping metal followed, sending chills up our backbones. It was as if a thousand fingernails were scraping down a blackboard.

"Oh shit, I think this is a real problem!" Marshall shouted. He had been thrown to the floor again, but he quickly staggered up and ran for the companionway a second time.

My head was pounding from the impact and things were fuzzy. I sat there for a second, stunned with disbelief. It took another few seconds to come to my senses and I was able to slowly crawl out of the aft cabin again. I grabbed the companionway rail and pulled myself up the stairs right behind him.

Marshall stepped out into the cockpit while I hesitated on the top stair. My heart was beating uncontrollably, and I had a terrible sick feeling in my stomach.

Marshall saw it first, a huge black mass with a dark red stripe at the water line smashed against our boat.

"What the hell is that?" he shouted. "The sail and the boom are blocking my view."

Bending down to get a better look, he gasped, "My God, it's a freighter! Where's Joe?"

We quickly scanned the cockpit for Joe. There was no sign of him.

With urgency in his voice, Marshall called to me, "The steering wheel and the rest of the cockpit appear to be intact except for one missing lazarette hatch. Dee, do you see Joe?"

I scanned the cockpit again.

"No, I don't see him." My voice trembled.

The lights from above instantly made it clear that we were dirty-dancing down the hull of a huge freighter, bumping, grinding, and thrashing all the way. The freighter, towering stories above us, was lit up like a Christmas tree. How could Joe not have seen it? Where the hell was Joe and where was the crew on the freighter? The ship was charging on as if no one was aware that it had hit us.

"Joe! Joe! Where are you, Joe?" Marshall shouted.

I echoed the same a moment later. There was no sound or sign of Joe anywhere. My heart felt as if it were going to beat a hole through my chest. Oh God! He must have been thrown overboard," I called to Marshall.

Although there was a lot of ambient light from the freighter, the sails cast a shadow on the cockpit area, giving it a surreal feeling and making it difficult to see the back of the cockpit clearly. Also, the steering wheel blocked both of our views of the far side.

While I stayed perched, unmoving, and silent, on the upper step of the companionway, Marshall moved around to the side of the helm and scanned the rear cockpit area again. He spotted Joe's feet sticking out of the lazarette. We heard a low gurgling sound at the same moment.

"What's that noise?" I shouted to Marshall.

Marshall gestured toward the back lazarette. "I think it's Joe. His head must be under water."

"Under water" I didn't understand. *How could that be?* .

The background noise of the freighter's engines and the screeching of the two vessels sliding against each other must have muffled any sounds he had been making before. I leaned over and could see he was stuck head-first in the lazarette, and somehow his head was indeed under water. I still didn't understand.

Marshall rushed over to muscle him out of the small compartment. With all the strength he could muster, he tried to pull Joe free, but Joe's shoulders were wedged below the opening.

He shouted back to me, "I don't know if I can get him out."

It was like a bad dream. I wanted to go help him but my legs were lead weights and I couldn't move.

"Keep trying," I urged him. Still feeling a little fuzzy, I put my hand up to my head and winced. My hair was wet and sticky. I knew I was bleeding.

Marshall's adrenaline was running high as he continued to struggle with Joe's dead weight. Somehow, somewhere, he found the extra strength to pull him free a few seconds later.

Joe obviously was in a state of semi-shock but capable of standing.

"Are you okay?" Marshall anxiously asked

Joe did not reply but nodded his head yes.

Knowing that Joe was safe, Marshall peered into the empty hole. As he did, the ambient light from the freighter illuminated the opalescent green of the ocean below. There should have been diving gear, extra lines, and all sorts of other equipment stored in the aft compartment, but he saw nothing between the water and us. The stern of our boat and everything stored there was gone.

There was no doubt in Marshall's mind that we were going to sink, and sink fast.

It took Marshall only a few seconds to assess the situation and take immediate control. I was still standing on the top step of the companionway stairs in a semi-trance, watching him rescue Joe. I had no idea of the severity of the problem, but I could hear Marshall's unflustered, controlled voice giving Joe and me commands.

"Grab the EPIRB (Emergency Position Indicating Radio beacon)," he ordered

Again, it felt like a dream; his voice seemed to come from so far away. I started to fiddle with the EPIRB release on the wall next to me, but without my glasses I couldn't see how to work the release.

"I can't get it undone," I yelled back.

He quickly reached over, undid the EPIRB release, and, seeming to act by rote, immediately activated the strobe and handed it to Joe. We knew a signal now was being sent via satellite to a NOAA tracking station dedicated to monitoring emergency transmissions, relating our exact latitude and longitude.

With an authoritatively calm voice Marshall instructed, "Whatever you do, Joe, be sure that this EPIRB gets into the life raft with us." Joe, staring numbly into space, still was in a state of shock but clutched the unit tightly and nodded that he understood.

"Dee, go below and send a Mayday over the single-sideband radio."

Marshall's apparent clear thinking and composure calmed me for a moment and I followed his orders. Normally, I'm not a passive first mate, but challenge his every suggestion with one of my own. That night my mind was capable of focusing only on insignificant details. I couldn't see the whole picture and I had no idea what to do next, so I did exactly what Marshall told me. Later he claimed it was the only time in our married life that I did.

I scrambled down the ladder and turned on the single sideband radio, but my panic returned as I frantically tried to remember the emergency channel. I couldn't remember, so I turned the knob to different stations, calling "Mayday, Mayday." I heard nothing. I punched a few of the preprogrammed channel buttons, still calling "Mayday, Mayday."

Nothing.

I knew I had to react quickly. *What is the emergency number? Shit, I can't remember.* I pushed more buttons, frantically calling "Mayday Mayday Mayday."

Silence.

I was so involved with the radio, I hadn't noticed that water was starting to come over the floorboards.

While I was trying to send out a call on the radio down below, Marshall sent out a Mayday on the VHF radio in the cockpit. Marshall knew time was limited. He looked down at the salon floor; the water had already risen three or four inches. He knew the radio would be dead in seconds.

"Dee, get out of there."

Miraculously, an unidentified voice responded on the VHF, saying it would track us. Marshall repeated our position.

He continued his last transmission. "We've been hit by a freighter. We're going down fast. We're going down now!"

The radio went dead.

The moment he finished his transmission, Marshall sent Joe and me forward to deploy our 12-foot inflated Zodiac dinghy, lashed forward of the mast with quick-release ties. Marshall knew he had to move quickly.

Time. I need more time. We don't have anything—passports, money—only the clothes on our back. If only we had our cash.

Marshall scrambled below to grab our cruising kitty of $15,000 stashed in three vacuum-sealed bags each containing fifty $100 bills.

I have to have enough time to grab the money.

The water was rising quickly. He was able to open the generator door and grab the cash we had so carefully hidden below. He turned and took five steps toward the companionway. A cushion floated by, impeding his exit. The water already was at his waist.

Man, this is going fast. Shit, we're out of time.

Marshall took one last look around as he swam toward the opening and pulled himself up the stairs.

All of a sudden, Marshall remembered with horror the turning block at the mast. He had added an extra line that neither Joe nor I knew about. At the last moment, before we left Puerto Vallarta, Marshall had added it as a precaution in case we got into extreme seas. It would keep the Zodiac from breaking free. He had wrapped the line through the turning block and back to the dinghy three times and then tied a series of three half-hitches on top.

Luckily, *Clambake* was sinking stern first, allowing Joe and me extra seconds to work on the Zodiac at the bow. Multiple lines with quick-release knots zigzagged the dinghy, securing it to the deck. My heart beat wildly as Joe and I worked in silence, forcing our minds to concentrate, forcing our fingers to respond, forcing ourselves not to panic.

I was having trouble with one of the quick-release knots, for the rope was jammed taut; my mind was telling my fingers to slowly pry it backward, but my fingers were trembling. I couldn't get it undone and I knew we were running out of time. Somewhere deep inside I was screaming, and damning our luck, and praying that we would live; and I was bargaining with God. *If only I can see my girls again, I promise I'll . . . I'll . . .*

I suddenly realized that Marshall hadn't gotten back up. I glanced up, looking for him. I knew it was only a few moments, but it seemed as if he had been gone a long time.

I looked away from the knot I was working on and glanced toward the back of the boat to see if he was there. There was no sign of him anywhere, and the back of the boat was sinking lower in the water every second.

Fearing the worst, I called to Joe, "I wonder what's taking Marshall so long? He should be back up by now. Joe, can you see Marshall? Do you think he has gotten trapped below?"

A million thoughts raced through my mind. *Should I leave the bow and try to find him? What do I do if he's trapped and I can't save him?* Then I saw him on the starboard side, slowly crawling forward. "Oh, thank God, there he is."

The boat was sinking faster and I forced my mind and fingers back to the knot. I turned one more time to look at Marshall and could tell immediately by his expression that something was terribly wrong. After all his clear thinking and quick assessment of the severity of the situation, he was chastising himself for not remembering that one crucial line sooner. He was just realizing that the one extra line that Joe and I couldn't see and didn't know about, could turn out to cause our demise.

By this time water was flowing over the decks. Marshall grabbed the lifeline to keep from slipping backward and being washed off the stern. I watched him slowly making his way forward, pulling himself with one hand on the lifelines while gripping the cash bags with the other.

The bow was almost perpendicular and *Clambake* was pulling us down as Joe and I frantically tried to untie the last lines and free our life raft. Just before we went under, I remember seeing Marshall lying on his stomach at the base of the mast. He was working frantically on that last line—the one that Joe and I didn't see or know about—as he disappeared with the boat.

Please, God, let him get it released.

I had no idea if he had been successful....

I was quickly snapped back to reality by our yacht transport's deep horn. It was time to join the crew and the other yacht owners in the cozy cafeteria on the third level for lunch. As we made our way to the upper deck, I thought back over the last five years. It was hard to believe so much time had passed since we first started across the ocean on this same voyage in our beloved *Clambake*.

We had been only 12 hours into our voyage and only 75 miles into our 3,000-mile journey when we experienced every sailor's ultimate nightmare: Everything we owned and had worked so hard for slipped beneath the sea in 90 terrifying seconds.

But this story didn't begin that night. It started 12 years earlier at a little lake in the Northern California mountains.

CHAPTER 2

Soulmate

NIGHT DESCENDED SOFTLY AS WE SAT QUIETLY CONVERSING, leaning up against a big old pine tree on the sandy shore of Lake Eagle. The air was still and the aroma of pine filled our nostrils. Across the way, a group of boaters were partying, but we were too busy planning our future to notice. We were here for a Hobie Cat regatta; however, that is not what we were discussing. We were tallying our assets and setting out goals on the brown paper shopping bag that held our weekend groceries. It was during this evening I became convinced of Marshall's determination for an early retirement. I had never met anyone with such definite aspirations for the future.

Ironically, his dreams were similar to my own, but unlike Marshall, I never had set specific goals to reach them. I listened enthusiastically and thought that maybe, with Marshall, it would be possible to achieve my childhood fantasy of traveling the world.

I had met Marshall just six months earlier, but felt as if I had known him all my life. We were soulmates.

I had been divorced for more than a year; my time was consumed with raising three daughters, and keeping up with their busy schedules, plus trying to make a living selling real estate. It left little or no time for pursuing romantic interests.

By chance we almost met at a bank. I say almost because although we spoke to each other, we were never formally introduced. I had popped into the bank to deposit a check from an escrow I had just closed.

While waiting in line I spotted Sally, a striking redhead, walking through the bank door. The jersey minidress she was wearing accentuated her natural curves and many males in the bank turned to look as she strolled over to get in line. I watched her enviously.

Sally also was in the real-estate business, working as an escrow officer for a title company I frequently used. A nice-looking gentleman accompanied her; *he* caught my eye immediately. He was of medium height with curly brown hair, a pleasant smile, and a physique bursting with hidden strength.

As I left, I stopped to chat. "Hi, Sally. How was your vacation?"

"Oh, hi, Dee. It was great. We had a really good time." She swung her long red locks over her shoulder.

"Where did you go?"

Flashing a big smile, she proceeded to tell me they flew into a fishing camp in a remote area of northern British Columbia.

"It was incredible," she continued, "The entire camp was on a float located at the end of a beautiful isolated inlet."

"Sounds fantastic. How was the fishing?"

"Unbelievable. We both got our limit. We're going to be eating salmon for awhile."

"Lucky you. I love salmon and I love to fish." I was envious as I chatted with Sally.

As I was about to leave, her friend smiled at me and with a captivating grin said, "It was nice to meet you, Dee. I'm impressed that you have one of those white deposit slips. I'm only familiar with the yellow withdrawal ones."

I was surprised and taken off guard, since Sally had made no effort to introduce us. I also was embarrassed by his comment and didn't know how to respond. Blushing, I muttered back, "It was nice to meet you, too."

I left the bank flustered. I wondered if it was his comment that had unnerved me. No, I decided, it was his incredible dancing blue eyes. They seemed to reach out and challenge me while at the same time reflected warmth and humor.

Somehow, he obtained my phone number and called me at work. I was out with clients and never returned his call. It wasn't that I didn't want to; I just never seemed to have enough time. I had thought about him several times since our encounter at the bank. He was the first man since my divorce that aroused my interest, but I figured he and Sally were involved in a serious relationship, so I put all thoughts of him out of my mind. Hours were precious and time couldn't be wasted on romantic dreams. I had to concentrate on closing transactions and putting food on the table for the four of us.

You can imagine my surprise when several days later I received a lease-option contract in the mail from Marshall, a lease for an hour for lunch with an option for *more to follow*. I couldn't resist accepting the invitation and spending a little time with a man who had such persistence and imagination; after all, I did have to eat once in a while. It was love at "first lunch," and I knew from that moment that Marshall was the man I wanted to spend the rest of my life with.

The following morning Marshall called me at work and asked, "Would you be interested in going to a Hobie Cat regatta this weekend?"

"That sounds like fun, but I've only been on a sailboat once in my life. I don't know anything about sailing."

"Don't worry about that. It's a piece of cake. If it's something you think you might enjoy, we can go out to the lake one afternoon this week and I can give you a quick lesson."

"I'll have to check with the girls' dad to see if he can take them for the weekend." I was stalling for time trying to decide whether I should accept. I was tempted to just say "yes". Even over the phone, his voice gave me the feeling that he was smiling flirtatiously.

"Why don't you see if you can work that out and I'll give you a call back later tonight."

"That sounds great," I responded, grateful for the extra time to make a decision.

I hung up the phone thinking, *What am I getting myself into?* Yet, I really wanted to go. Racing sounded like fun and I had always wanted to learn to sail. Besides, there was something about Marshall that made me feel safe. He was easy to talk to; I felt as if we were old friends. *Strange,* I thought, *after only one lunch.* But I reminded myself that lunch had lasted all afternoon.

I was able to arrange for the girls to stay with their father for the weekend. When Marshall called, I excitedly accepted. I still had mixed emotions. I was eager to spend more time with Marshall, but I was nervous about an entire weekend—and one spent racing a sailboat, no less.

We left Friday night towing the Hobie Cat behind his Cherokee Chief. We packed an ice chest full of food and drinks, took sleeping bags, and planned to use the Hobie Cat as our camping site. He explained that most of the other racers would be doing the same.

Saturday morning before the race began, we walked the famous long Monterey pier. As we walked past a group of colorful flags, Marshall pointed to the red triangle and casually mentioned, "Well, this should be an interesting morning."

"What do you mean?" I asked.

With that captivating twinkle in his eye and a smile I couldn't resist, he grabbed my hand and replied, "You'll see."

Before the race Marshall gave me a few quick lessons on tacking and jibing and what else was expected of me during the competition. We would be wearing what they called "diapers," a colorful nylon wrap that resembled a diaper but had a big steel hook in the front. This hook, I was instructed, I would attach to another hook and cable, which was attached to the mast. We would hook in when we were sailing to weather.

"What is sailing to weather?" I asked.

Smiling, he shrugged as if it was no big deal and patiently said, "Sailing to weather just means sailing into the wind."

It was time to suit up into our wetsuits. The first race was minutes away and some of the other boats already were milling around the starting line. I felt little butterflies in my stomach as I looked at the waves cresting not far from shore. We had only practiced in calm lake waters; these waves looked huge in comparison.

I also noticed that we were the only co-ed team racing on the 18-foot Hobies. All of the other competing teams were pairs of men. I was 5-foot 5-inches tall, very athletic and competitive, but I only weighed 118 pounds. Looking at the other crews, it appeared weight and strength might be a consideration. I wondered why Marshall had chosen me for his crew. I thought that I was beginning to understand what he meant when he said this day should prove interesting.

We shoved the Hobie off the beach, hopped aboard, and quickly joined the other racers. We jockeyed for the best position, dodging and darting among the other boats. I was in awe at Marshall's maneuvering capabilities, especially within such close proximity. There were several instances when I let out a yell, closed my eyes, and prepared for a collision, but he quickly proved I was with no amateur sailor. We never even scraped another boat, though I know that sometimes we were just inches apart.

The starting gun went off . . . and I found out what that hook was for. I followed Marshall's instructions and hooked in as a gust of wind hit us. Our hull rose sharply out of the water. Marshall yelled a "Wahoo!" as we flew by the other boats, taking the lead.

"Boy, are we going fast," I yelled to him as I felt the spray brush against my cheek. "What do I do now?"

"Just hang on and I'll let you know when we're going to tack," he instructed over the howling wind.

We rounded the course, tacking and jibing. I found myself trying to dig my toenails into the hull as I was doing my best to *hang on*. I also found that talking to myself helped alleviate my constant fear that something disastrous was about to happen.

Twenty feet from the finish line and just seconds before we crossed it in first place, a strong gust of wind hit us. Marshall yelled for me to hook in, but I responded too slowly. The hull rose and a huge wave came over the top of the pontoons and lifted my feet off the trampoline. I toppled off the boat, and the boat flipped over! We managed to upright her fairly quickly and hop back aboard. Unbelievably, we still were able to pass the finish line in third position.

The four remaining races over the next two days were just as exciting. Small-craft warnings had been issued; there was a lot of wind, and as I looked out over the bay, I could see four- to five-foot swells. It was going to be a weekend that would definitely challenge Marshall's skills and my bravery.

In the second race we pitchpoled as the boat did a cartwheel through the water and I went sailing through the air in my trapeze far out in front of the boat.

In the third race we turtled, turning the boat upside down. The mast started to fill with water. We tried to right the boat but were unable to do so because of the weight of the water in the mast. We both treaded water, waiting for help to arrive, as waves broke over the boat and us. I started to shiver, partly from the cold water and partly from fear. I tried willing the waves to be even higher so they would help push the Hobie upright. I didn't realize at the time that higher waves would be useless on the heavy mast. It seemed like an eternity until assistance came.

The rescue boat was unable to reach the righting line and inadvertently used the main sheet to right us. Consequently, when we finally were pulled upright, the sails filled in and the boat took off. Marshall was unable to slow us down because the main sheet was still tied to the rescue boat. He had managed to pull himself aboard, but I was still underneath, clutching onto the dolphin bar, trying to remember what was at the back of the boat if I let go.

At first Marshall didn't realize I was still hanging on under the boat.

I yelled to him in between gulps of air and seawater. "Marshall . . . (gulp). Marshall . . . (gulp)."

"Where the hell are you?"

"I'm under . . . (gulp) . . . the trampoline. Can you stop this thing?"

He called to the rescue boat to cut the line and then yelled to me, "Just let go and I'll catch you as you drift to the back of the boat."

Right, I thought. *No way.* "Is there anything at the back . . . gulp . . . of the boat that can chop me up if I let go?"

I felt the boat slow down as he released the main sheet and turned the boat into the wind.

"No, there's nothing that can hurt you. Just trust me; I'll catch you."

Hobbie Cat racing in the early days.

I was silent for a moment as I mulled this over. "I'm shark bait," I muttered to myself. I was beginning to wonder if I would ever see my girls again.

"Are you still there, Dee?"

"Yes, but I'm afraid to let go," I yelled back.

"I promise I'll catch you. You'll do just fine," he assured me one more time.

I closed my eyes, took a big breath of air, said my prayers, and released my death grip on the bars. In seconds I felt his strong arms lifting me onto the boat. Not only did he rescue me, he also managed to steer the boat into the wind so we wouldn't capsize again. It was what I later referred to as my 40-mile-an-hour douche!

We came in third overall that glorious and terrifying weekend. Marshall was impressed that I was still smiling at the end of it. He didn't realize I was smiling because I was happy I was still alive, but he had decided that anyone who persevered through that weekend was definitely someone he wanted to get to know a lot better.

From that weekend on, we spent almost every possible spare moment together.

Marshall loved sailing and I loved the water, so through our courting days it was natural that we took up the weekend sport of Hobie Cat-racing and found ourselves spending every weekend at the local lake. That was great because it was a family event that included the girls. They loved camping, bonfires, and watching "cute boys" at the lake. Marshall and I loved the competitive fun of racing.

Occasionally during our dating days, the girls would spend a weekend with their father, giving Marshall and me time alone. Six months into our courtship, this was one of those precious weekends. The setting at a beautiful lake in the mountains away from work and phones was perfect. The fraternizing and racing during the day was fun and challenging, but we were enjoying our time alone in the evenings. I loved listening to Marshall's tales of his previous sailing adventures to Hawaii and the South Pacific. I knew they were embellished to impress me, but I didn't mind. I *was* impressed; this had always been my dream, too. I had always wanted to be a recreational director on an ocean liner, but the life he was telling me about would certainly do as a close second.

This weekend was no different with the tales, but there was a determination that was new. He had a dream, and my feet-on-the-ground attitude didn't stand a chance pitted against his vision of the future. He wanted an early retirement for us, but not one spent in the garden or at a bridge table. Instead, we'd be cruising from one palm tree and sandy beach to the next in Tahiti, New Zealand, and Australia. He knew exactly what kind of sailboat we'd have: About 50-feet long, built for speed as well as safety, with an aft cockpit and three staterooms. He had envisioned it clearly for years.

That evening at Lake Eagle, we set our goals and devised a strict savings program that included only camping vacations, budget restaurants, and shopping sprees for boat items, not clothes. The race was on to save: The carrot was a boat; the finish line was Tahiti.

Not long after that weekend we combined families—his daughter and my three daughters —and moved into his home in the mountains. We opened a real-estate business in the small retirement community of Shingletown, California. Now we were living, working, and playing together, and I had never been happier or felt as if life could be more perfect.

CHAPTER 3

Building the Dream

SEVERAL YEARS FLEW BY. I REMEMBER THEM AS BE-
ING similar to an ocean crossing: 97 percent boring with
a *mission,* and three percent white-knuckle.

That is not quite accurate. Life with Marshall was never
boring. He was full-time entertainment. Some days he was like
a billiard ball bouncing off the walls. I was never quite sure
what direction he was going next, verbally or physically. He
would wake up in the morning literally bouncing. I would open
my eyes to a nude form bellowing over me, jumping up and
down on our waterbed, beating his hairy chest and yelling for
all our neighbors to hear, "Feed me, feed me."

It was difficult not to smile. My day started by being bounced
out of bed.

Months continued to flow into years. The only memorable
days were the Sundays we spent at Whiskeytown Lake with our
local yacht club racing our Hobie. As friendships developed and
grew stronger, so did the competitiveness. Marshall became
known for his unconventional dip starts and unorthodox diver-
sions. He would go to great lengths to distract the competition
prior to the start of the race while everyone was jockeying for
the best starting position.

One weekend in particular, I remember his blasting out the music from the movie "Flash Dance" on our boombox while he encouraged me to stand at the mast and pantomime a pole dance until the starting gun went off.

That same day Marshall started high on the wrong side of the starting line coming across on a beam reach. Because he was alone and in totally clean air, he gained incredible speed as he approached the line. He waited until the last minute and just before the starting gun went off, found a hole in the fleet, dipped below the line, and came out like a slingshot with clean air and a couple of boat lengths ahead of everyone else. The start was daring; timing was crucial. There was always the risk that if Marshall was not able to find a hole in the fleet to dip below the line before the starting gun went off, we would wind up beginning the race in last position.

This particular weekend, the start was successful, and we won the race. One of our good friends, Joe, came in just seconds behind us.

As Joe crossed the finish line he called out to Marshall, "How about a race back to the marina?"

Marshall agreed with a grin, "Sure, let's do it."

Joe was a good sailing friend. He loved life and lived it to the fullest, sometimes taking risks that had gained him a reputation for being accident-prone. However, he was an inspiration to be around and his enthusiasm for packing each day full of new experiences was contagious. He was an excellent sailor and a formidable opponent; Marshall always enjoyed a challenge against him.

Both captains pulled in their mainsails and headed toward the marina. At the last moment and just before reaching the entrance, Marshall let out the main sheet and fell off the wind, heading straight for the logs that formed the breakwater.

Joe, realizing what Marshall was going to do, shouted, "You can't do that."

Marshall, laughing, yelled back, "Watch me."

Marshall quickly called for me to pull up the daggerboards and get as far back on the trampoline as possible. Before I realized what he was doing, we had crossed over the top of the logs and landed in the marina ahead of Joe.

Marshall, laughing heartily, yelled back to Joe, "I think I just beat you for the second time today."

All Joe could say was, "Not fair." But he was shaking his head and laughing too.

During those *mission* years of trying to make enough money to retire early and reach our cruising goal, we changed boats several times. We moved up from the Hobie to a 27-foot racing catamaran called a Stiletto. This gave us a new lift to life. It was bigger, faster, and required more crew than our Hobie Cat, so it gave us a new temporary focus to keep us going. Our dream of a 50-foot boat and Tahiti was still out there, but the real estate market had taken a down turn, and rearing four girls was very expensive. We were moving toward our goal more slowly than we had planned.

As more years trickled by, we sold the Stiletto and bought a monohull Olson 25. Again, the new boat worked like a little booster shot. She kept us going, but always with the dream of Tahiti in the future. We still camped, but racing had become more of a family effort, with the girls and sometimes their boyfriends, helping us crew. The hope of an early retirement and a 50-foot boat still was our dream, but the real estate market slowed even more.

As part of our plan for early retirement, we had continuously purchased pieces of property. Some had fairly good-sized payments. Our ultimate financial goal was to convert our properties into rentals that we would own free and clear and would provide us retirement income. Initially, this meant hefty payments until we were able to pay down the loans and ultimately see positive cash flow.

Business had become so slow that there were several months when we worried we were not going to be able to meet all of our financial obligations, but somehow at the last minute we found ways to make every one of them. I can remember vividly one desperate month when we had to sell an antique slot machine to make one of the land payments. Not long after that, a somber Marshall sat across from me.

"I have called everyone I can possibly think of and I have no idea how to make one more sale," he said. "I think to survive we are going to have to go back into my old business of the dental laboratory."

Before I met Marshall, he had lived in Hawaii and had owned two dental laboratories. It was tedious work but he was successful at it. One day for fun, we calculated how many teeth Marshall had made in his career. It turned out to be more than 35,000. It was obvious why he wasn't very excited about going back into the business, but now we had no choice. Real estate activity had slowed so much we had to make a change or close our doors to survive.

Within a month we opened a dental laboratory in the back room of our real estate office and were providing mail orders to his old accounts in Hawaii.

Years ticked by as we put in long hours trying to make ends meet and raise our four girls. With Marshall's dental career, we were able to survive those slow years while a lot of competitors closed their doors. We kept our doors open; we just wore two hats. We never gave up on our goal, and continued to dream of the day we would own our 50-footer.

That day seemed to drift further and further into the future.

Finally, in the mid 80's the real estate market started to improve and we again started reading boat ads. One day, I saw an ad in a popular sailing magazine that caught my eye. "Will trade 50-foot boat for real estate." Because we had accumulated quite a few properties over the years, this ad sounded appealing. We made the call.

CHAPTER 4

Fate and Tragedy Intervene

THE BOAT WAS LOCATED IN VENTURA, CALIFORNIA, AND HER name was *Clambake*. I had a long conversation with the owner. "She is exactly what we have been searching for," I told Marshall as calmly as I could after I hung up the phone.

We agreed to see her the following weekend; it would be a six-hour trip down the coast, but we could use a weekend away.

The moment we saw *Clambake* we knew she was "our boat." She was a Tayana 52 aft- cockpit performance cutter designed by Robert Perry. Light beige with a brown stripe, she looked sleek and sexy nestled in her berth. As I descended the cockpit stairs, I caught my breath; she was gorgeous. The main salon was bright and airy, decorated in the popular mauve colors and appointed with incredibly beautiful teak staving. Aft of the companionway she had two ample staterooms. The spacious U-shaped galley was port side, while a head and chart table were starboard. Forward was the main salon with a gorgeous round teak dinette table with inlaid wood and a circular settee surrounding it. Across from the dinette was a slightly curved long plush couch. Forward was another head and the master stateroom with an oversized double berth.

As the owner showed us around we realized she had minimal navigation equipment but a good sail inventory, complete with a spinnaker that the owner never used. She was powered with a Perkins 4-236 85-horsepower diesel engine, and had a 5-kilowatt Onan generator. During the sea trial she performed like magic, responding quickly to all of Marshall's drills. He was particularly impressed with her nimbleness in maneuvering and her quick acceleration after tacking in a light breeze. We swear she sighed, "Choose me," when we left her at the dock.

Yes, a real estate trade would work fine for the seller; however, they were living aboard with two small children and would have to move immediately into the traded property. This created a problem, because we had renters in the property. Then we found out the sellers didn't have enough money to move into temporary quarters until the transaction closed. This was getting complicated, and we were beginning to wonder if we could make this work.

We finally were able to negotiate a $1,000 advance moving allowance and arranged for them to stay in a guesthouse on our property in Shingletown for a couple of weeks. They were to move into their house when the renters moved out. After working out these obstructions, things appeared to be falling into place. Three weeks later, in March 1985, we signed a huge stack of papers to purchase *Clambake,* promising, "Till death do us part."

As our daughters left the roost to go off to college, our vow of poverty swelled the cruising kitty. It allowed us to lavish our new dependent with the latest in marine fashions: Radar, watermaker, GPS, sails, VHF and HAM radios, dinghy, and on and on. No expense, no effort, no sacrifice was spared. This included our 1,000-mile commute. We lived in Shingletown, California and *Clambake* lived in Seattle, Washington. We tore up and down the freeway making a 12-hour commute whenever we could escape from the office. For five years we dreamed of the day we'd be counting islands instead of exits.

At this point, we considered a career change. Marshall always believed that if you were successful and disciplined in one business, you could succeed in another. So, approximately a year after we purchased *Clambake*, I popped the question on one of our 6 a.m. to 6 p.m. commutes.

"What would you think of going into the charter business with our new boat?"

"Sounds interesting, but do you think we could make any money?"

"Sure we could." I was always enthusiastic and never chose to see any of the negatives when proposing new ideas to Marshall. This was my mother's influence. She taught me to think that I could do anything if I tried.

When I was a little girl, she became very upset with me if she ever heard me say: "I can't do it." She would lash out that she never wanted to hear me say those words again. Then she would sing a little ditty that she made up: "I can do it. I can do it, if I try." I can't begin to tell you how many times I heard that song while growing up.

It may have been a form of brainwashing, but it was powerful. Later in life, I always knew that if I wanted something badly enough, I had to keep trying and eventually I could make it happen. It never crossed my mind or occurred to me that I wouldn't be able to do it. I just assumed I could.

"You would be the captain and I would be the cook," I continued.

"Well, you *are* a gourmet cook; everybody loves your cooking," Marshall agreed. "It does sound like fun, and we'd be doing what we love every day. To be honest, I'm really getting bored with the real estate business."

As the discussion continued, Marshall took the side of the devil's advocate. He was always the more conservative and cautious one in our business decisions, although he never showed that side of himself around the office, or for that matter in front of our friends. He was always throwing our associates into a frenzy with his off-the-wall comments, jokes, or pranks. It was his way of keeping our sales force motivated, and it did seem to keep them on their toes. However, this was a serious discussion that went on for most of the 12-hour commute.

By the time we reached home we had decided to research the idea further. We decided to even go so far as to have brochures made up and to attend a boat show in Victoria, British Columbia, that was exclusively for charter-boat brokers to preview charter boats and their crews.

The Victoria Charter Boat Show was in September; all the big names in the business were there, including Lynn Jackney, Bev Fisher, and Gail O'Hern. The brokers seemed to like *Clambake* and us and promised some sure bookings for the next season. On the way home we decided that if we were going to make a career change the following summer, we needed to start making arrangements to sell our real estate business and prepare for the transition.

October was a busy month at the office. Business was good and we also began to prepare for the transition. Things appeared to be going all too smoothly both at work and on the home front with our daughters. I had the ominous feeling this good fortune couldn't last.

We had been home from the boat show only a couple of weeks when we got the devastating phone call. It was late in the evening and we had just crawled into bed exhausted when the phone rang.

"Who would be calling us at this hour?" I asked Marshall. "I hope it's not one of the girls."

I waited impatiently while Marshall picked up the phone. He was silent and expressionless as he listened. He finally muttered a quiet "uh-umm . . . uh-umm."

"Who is it?" I frantically questioned him; I realized there was a problem.

He didn't answer but continued to listen. Watching his face, I could tell that something terrible had happened. I felt that dreadful sick feeling in my stomach.

"Who is it?" I asked again, my voice trembling.

"It's Tiffany . . . she's dead," he snapped back.

I was immobile, speechless. I couldn't believe what I was hearing. How could that be? We had talked to her two nights ago on the phone. She had complained of the flu and was going to the doctor. What could have happened?

It seemed like just yesterday that Tiffany had come to Marshall and asked if she could live with us. She was only 12, but she decided she couldn't handle living with her stepfather any longer. She had threatened to run away. She had been living with her mother and her mother's new husband in Los Angeles since the divorce courts had awarded Marshall's ex-wife custody.

We knew that we would have to go to court, because Tiffany's mother was not about to give her up without a fight. It was a difficult time for all of us. Emotions ran high but it was important to follow through and do what was best for Tiffany at the time.

The court granted Tiffany her wish to live with her father after the judge interviewed her in his private chambers for more than an hour. He told us later he had questioned Tiffany from every direction possible to test the validity of her request. He was very impressed that a child her age was so mature and had so much determination. I can often remember teasing Tiffany that she didn't have the word *no* in her vocabulary, only different shades of *yes*. She knew exactly what she wanted in life and had incredible resolve to obtain it. A trait passed on to her from her father.

She moved in with us in our mountain home right after the trial. There was definitely an adjustment time for all of us. She was used to being an only child and now had to share her dad's attention with three sisters.

Tiffany was a petite five-footer. She had been diagnosed with Turner's syndrome shortly after birth, so we knew she never would grow taller or be able to have children, two of the effects of the syndrome.

I will always envision her the night of her junior prom. We were waiting in the car outside the school when I spotted her gliding down the sidewalk. She looked like a little fairy princess in her flowing pink gown. Her dark brown hair bobbed in the breeze and her beautiful big brown eyes sparkled with excitement. She bubbled with life and spirit; you could tell by looking at her she was having the time of her life.

Her incredible memory always amazed, but at the same time, lovingly irritated me. She could read an article once and remember all the facts, including the names, a task very difficult for me. She was a natural with foreign languages and always did well at school—so well, in fact, that she graduated early and spent her senior year in France as an exchange student.

She idolized her father and while living with her mother, had missed him and their previous lifestyle. As a family, they had lived aboard sailboats in Hawaii from the time Tiffany was three years old. She loved sailing and anything around the water. Marshall frequently told stories about her cruising around the harbor in her own Sabot sailboat when she was a little girl, visiting with other boaters. Everyone knew Tiffany.

I was snapped back to the reality of the situation as I watched Marshall hang up the phone.

"What happened?" I asked softly.

"Tiffany's dead," he yelled back. Fear and anger were reflected in his voice.

"How?" I was numb with disbelief.

"I don't know." His shoulders slumped and he shook his head from side to side. "Her mother found her dead on the bathroom floor when she got home from work."

I didn't know what to do or say, yet felt I had to do something. The whole thing seemed surreal; it had to be a mistake. I knew what Marshall was telling me was true; I just didn't want to believe it.

I pried the phone from Marshall's hand and dialed each of the girl's numbers and then their grandparents'. I can't remember what I said to them, but I had to do something at the moment and that seemed natural and rational.

I finally hung up the phone and grabbed Marshall. We sat there on the bed holding each other, rocking back and forth with tears streaming down our cheeks, sobbing uncontrollably.

The cause of death was myocarditis. It was sudden. All plans were put on hold. We felt we couldn't breathe or function. How could one of our children die before us? I was in a state of terrible depression, for I loved Tiffany as I did one of my own daughters, but for Marshall it was worse. Marshall had not just lost his only daughter; he also had lost his first mate and the only person he had left with whom to share all those early sailing memories—their sailing experiences in the Hawaiian Islands and especially, their trip to the South Pacific. Tiffany was his tie to his past. It was as if his entire past, in an instant, had been sunk beneath him.

The following weeks were consumed with the funeral and all the incredible emotions that go along with losing a child: The inconceivable emptiness, the guilt that there might have been something we could have done to prevent her death, and the anger that she was taken from us. We missed her terribly. We still do. There isn't a day in our lives when something doesn't trigger some memory of Tiffany.

After Tiffany's death, we couldn't muster up enthusiasm to begin a new career in sailboat chartering. We gave up that idea and continued in real estate, a career we knew and did well in and could pretty much continue in our depressed state. Tiffany's death drove us to a new intensity even while we mourned her. We buried our thoughts and sadness in our work and concentrated on making money. Life was fragile and we didn't want to waste a lot of precious years dreaming.

We went on an even stricter financial diet at home. With all of the girls in college, we sold our main home and moved into a one-room guest cabin on adjoining property we owned. While our business peers and friends were buying large homes, new cars, and various other state-of-the-art fun toys, we concentrated on paying down our loans. We continued driving our old Ford pickup truck and camper and scrimping wherever we could.

We had been used to living frugally during slow times. Now that we again were making money, we found it easy to sock every extra dollar we made into paying off our investment loans in a new determination to reach our goal and reach it fast.

Occasionally, there was the ego issue and we were tempted to stray from our goal. Now that the real estate market had improved, it was sometimes difficult to watch friends or peers lavish rewards of success upon themselves while we had nothing to show for our accomplishment that our friends could see. Unfortunately, paying off loans wasn't fun or sexy. You couldn't see and touch a loan that was paid down as you could a brand-new car or motor home, but we were on a mission.

For almost four years, we lived in a one-room cabin that didn't have a kitchen big enough to hold a refrigerator—we had to keep it on our back deck. All that time we drove our 1972 Ford pickup, with its worn-out shock absorbers, and enviously admired our friends' shiny new cars and big homes.

At age 45, we decided to retire. That was one of our hardest decisions, because it was difficult to determine when and if we really had enough money.

For months we spent many a night in the hot tub doing what we called verbally masturbating—in other words, doing all the *what ifs* we could possibly think of.

"What if we sell the business, take off sailing, and five years down the road run out of money?" I asked Marshall.

"Well, even if times get tough, as long as we own our rentals free and clear, we have the ability to reduce the rents and be more competitive if the rental market gets tight; and if we really need to save more money, we can come home for awhile and manage our units ourselves instead of having a property manager do it for us."

"It would really be hard to start all over if something disastrous happened."

Marshall teased back, "Trust me, nothing ever happens to me. I have the Colgate® tooth paste invisible shield around me; I'll protect you."

"Right," I grimaced, thinking of some of the minor catastrophes he'd already had while playing some practical jokes and just being Marshall.

We finally concluded that the answer is that you never have enough money. You always have the ability to spend more than you make, but discipline and a dream can make it possible to adjust your lifestyle to the amount you have. Here is where the issue of priorities comes in.

For years we had planned together what we wanted. We had envisioned the freedom to sail to wherever we chose and stay for as long as we wanted. Our dream was here. We agreed that doing it *now* was important; how lavishly we furnished our sailboat didn't matter. Now the only question we asked each other was, "Do we have the courage to do it?"

CHAPTER 5

The Dream Becomes Reality

IN JANUARY 1991 WE DECIDED TO SELL OUR BUSINESS AND our home. Our children threw a huge surprise retirement party. Our family, friends, and peers were there. It was an incredible party with about 70 people attending. The girls arranged for us to meet at a local restaurant on the pretense that they were treating Marshall to a birthday dinner.

As we walked through the door, Marshall and I couldn't believe our eyes. Our mouths dropped open in total surprise. Our entire sales force and a lot of other business associates, old sailing friends, numerous family members, and a host of old friends greeted us.

The girls had decorated the room in a Bon Voyage party atmosphere, with streamers and balloons. Around the perimeter they had hung picture groupings reflecting different eras of our life together. One wall was dedicated to sailing, with photos of all our different boats from racing days. There were pictures of the Hobie Cat, the Stiletto, and the Olson 25. There were pictures of Marshall and me on the Hobie flying a hull and another of us receiving a trophy at one of the regattas.

Another wall was devoted to our real estate business. There were images of our office crew and of the old office building. There was one photo of Marshall and me hammering in a "Sold" sign.

The last wall was devoted to a world map surrounded by pictures of gorgeous beaches with palm trees, exotic-looking islands surrounded with crystal blue water, and all sorts of banners with all the clichés bestowed on sailors as they are about to embark on a voyage.

As we mingled among the guests we were inundated with questions about our plans. Over and over we heard various versions of why others could never do what we were doing. They would ask, "How long are you going to be gone? How far do you plan to go? Do you plan to go all the way around the world?"

We always answered, "We'll keep on going as long as we're having fun. When it ceases to be fun, we'll return home."

That seemed to produce an interesting response, usually something reflecting a slight disapproval of irresponsibility to our family, profession, or society in general.

One old friend responded, "I just don't know how you can do this. I know I never could; I would miss the kids too much."

Another uttered, "I couldn't stand being with Frank on a 24-hour basis with no place to escape."

And yet another, looking at us sympathetically, told us, "I'd be bored to tears. What on earth will you do all day confined on a *boat?*"

It was difficult for a lot of our friends and peers to understand how we could leave everything—especially family—and go off and live on a small boat without any conveniences, just bobbing around the ocean.

Marshall and I often discussed our ultimate destination in

our hot-tub sessions, but we decided and agreed we wanted to stick to our original goal of freedom to go wherever we wanted and stay as long as we wanted. We didn't want to be tied to a schedule of having to be somewhere at a specific month or time. Nor did we want to commit to telling everyone we were going to circumnavigate the globe and then feel obligated to do just that, even though we weren't enjoying it.

As the evening progressed, they had the typical roast that goes along with most retirement parties—all those embarrassing moments and stories we would love to forget but that they all loved to tell over and over.

Our agents loved to tell the story, and of course one of them did that night, of the day that Marshall tried to prove that it was always possible to get a client. Marshall had just finished one of his motivational office meetings. The theme was that one needs to be creative in order to be successful. Just as he finished his speech, one of our competitors stepped into our office to pick up a key. Marshall walked out of our office as Don, the other agent, walked in. Marshall went over to Don's car, introduced himself to the clients, and asked them to go along with a little joke for just a few minutes. He told them they had a great agent, but that sometimes we needed to get his heart rate up first thing in the morning to get him going.

Marshall hopped into the car with the clients, drove a little way down the street, and ultimately did a U-turn and brought the clients back. In the meantime, our poor competitor, Don, stood in our office doorway staring with his mouth agape at his car and his clients disappearing down the street with Marshall behind the wheel.

When Marshall returned, Don, his face still red from his rising blood pressure, went out to meet them. Marshall hopped out of the car, turned to Don, and with that mischievous grin of his, blurted out for all to hear, "Gee, Don, your clients are really great folks, and your car isn't bad, either." Our agents almost rolled on the floor with laughter. They talked about that day for years.

It was a great party, and we couldn't believe our kids had organized this huge affair without our knowing about it. It was with mixed emotions of awe and perhaps a little envy that our friends sent us off that evening with wishes of "Good luck and smooth sailing." We knew a few thought we were crazy to leave a successful business at such an early age. Maybe they even wished that we might fail in our dream.

At the close of the evening we stood by the door, thanking our guests as they left. Several stopped to congratulate us again and shake our hands. As they stood there shaking their heads in disbelief, they would reiterate what had been said so many times before that evening: "I don't know how you can do it; I don't know how you can walk away from such a successful business at such an early age."

We'd merely smile and say, "You know how it is when you get older; you start to lose a few brain cells." We knew they would never understand our commitment to our dream.

Luckily our family supported us, and although they knew it would be difficult with us off in different corners of the earth, they unselfishly encouraged us to pursue our dream. We were hoping that they would join us in different parts of the world.

It took just a few short weeks to put things in storage and load the U-haul for the last 12-hour commute up the freeway. We moved everything of value to us into the van to go to the boat and packed everything else into boxes to store in the garage until we returned. It wasn't a dream any longer; it was reality, and we were ready to make *Clambake* our permanent home.

The day finally came for us to begin the 12-hour commute for the last time. We were exhausted when we arrived in Anacortes, Washington, where the boat was moored, so we decided not to unpack anything until the following day. It seemed strange that evening to go down below into our beautiful boat and think, *This is now home.*

It didn't take long to organize things. In a short time we were able to sit down, kick back, and analyze what we had just done.

Marshall looked across at me and asked, "Well, how do you feel about your new home?"

"I was thinking about that same thing and about to ask *you* that very question." I stopped for a moment to consider exactly how I felt. "Well, I can tell you after four years of cooking in that tiny kitchen in our cabin, I'm going to be in heaven in my galley. I really think I'm absolutely going to love living aboard."

"Oh, good. I was worried once we really got here that you wouldn't feel that way."

"Why did you think that?"

"Oh, I don't know. It's just that I've lived aboard before and know what it's like, and I thought maybe you might be having second thoughts."

"Not in the least. I think I'm going to feel very secure in our new home and just love this new lifestyle. It's hard to explain, but I feel as if a huge burden has just been lifted off my shoulders. Do you feel that way?"

"I always feel that way on a boat. Living aboard gives me the feeling of self-sufficiency and independence. I know the problems we encounter on the boat are real ones that we can usually solve on our own. The fact that we don't have to rely on a decision of the bureaucracy as we so often did in real estate brings me great peace of mind and the feeling of freedom. I know that living on a boat isn't always ideal, but it sure gives me a secure feeling."

The next few weeks flew by. One day disappeared into the next as we worked on a gazillion little projects to make the boat cruise-ready. We loved living full time in the marina and enjoyed the camaraderie we were able to share with other boaters we met.

The boat was becoming an enjoyment that made us feel young and adventurous again. We often would take off in the dinghy late in the afternoon after the projects for the day were completed, and poke around the island into new nooks and crannies. There was something about the islands that always seemed to beckon to us to peek around just one more corner.

We had planned to cruise in the inland waterways of British Columbia the first summer and then head down the coast in late August or early September. All of the family was coming up to the islands to join us at different times throughout the summer. We looked forward to some quality time with each of them.

The summer flew by and before we knew it, August was here. This was the month we tentatively had scheduled to head down the coast. We had become familiar with the use of the radar, the radio, and the GPS and felt comfortable with their operation. They were mounted in our cockpit for easy viewing under way. We had installed a ham radio at our navigation station down below and both of us had gotten our ham licenses. Our aluminum radar reflector had been mounted on the mast. A watermaker was installed. Our sail inventory was complete and new roller furling for the jib had been added. The engine oils and filters had been changed. All of our running gear and lights were operational.

Our 12-foot Zodiac with its 25hp engine was secured on our forward deck. It doubled as our life raft and was provisioned with a grab bag with freeze-dried food, a water still, fishing gear, solar blankets, and emergency flares, first aid, and safety gear. I had made a tent out of Sunbrella cloth to cover the dinghy, so that if we ever needed to use it for a life raft, we would have protection from the el-

Heading south in the Straits of Juan de Fuca aboard Clambake *on our voyage.*

ements. The life sling and man-overboard pole were secured to the back rail; life jackets with whistles and automatic lights were hung in the companionway for easy access. We had purchased the last group of charts and guidebooks.

We finally agreed that the boat was equipped for the trip and we were ready to cut the dock lines and begin our journey. We called the kids to let them know we were planning on leaving the following week. They all showed up to spend the weekend with us. It was hard kissing everyone goodbye, but we were eager to start our journey. Tears rolled down our cheeks as we untied the dock lines and drifted out of our slip.

"You guys be very careful out there. Stay in touch a lot so we know where you are and that you are okay," yelled our eldest daughter Sheri, as we started to pull away.

"Good luck, have fun, and . . . be careful!" yelled the others.

We nodded *yes* we would and continued to wave until they were specks in the distance as we drifted out the main channel.

We headed out the Strait of Juan De Fuca and down the west coast, watching Washington, Oregon, and California slip by on the radar. We enjoyed various ports along the way and especially talking with locals at the quaint seaside harbors and pubs.

We took a break for a couple of weeks when we reached San Francisco Bay. The family came to visit to make sure we were doing okay. It was great having all of them with us again, and fun to take in the sights and sounds of the city, especially from the water. We hoped they could find time to join us from time to time as we continued our travels.

We soon tired of the city's bright lights, expensive restaurants, and the constant sound of sirens in the distance. We longed to be out on the water again and back into some quaint, quiet harbors. We continued our journey down the California coast.

Crossing the Mexican border was a major milestone for us. The coastline was beautiful and the sun felt warm on our skin as *Clambake* cut smoothly through the water. We watched the shoreline quickly slide by, and it wasn't long before we could see the sea buoys marking the entrance to our first foreign port, Ensenada, Mexico. We were every bit as proud as Cortez or Balboa was of their discoveries. They may have been first, but they were long dead, and we were a class of new explorers. We were just beginning to live and discover. Life didn't get any better than this.

CHAPTER 6

Life Is Good

B AJA AND THE SEA OF CORTEZ WERE IDYLLIC. THERE WERE
hundreds of wonderful anchorages surrounded by sleepy,
picturesque fishing villages. Most were very laid back; the men
fished for a living and women took care of the family at home.

A good number of the villages didn't have electricity or re-
frigeration. It was common to see lines of fish drying along the
roadside. As we walked their dirt roads, we watched children
playing amongst goats and chickens, all meandering in and out
of open doorways.

Observing the folks living in these villages, we realized
that although their lives were simple and they were poor in
material possessions, they had a richness of life and the children seemed happy. We never heard a baby crying, and there
appeared to be true concern and love for each other. The combination of the simple life, the abundance of sea life close by,
and the beauty of the world all around gave them the quality of
life we all search for.

As we traveled from one spectacular anchorage to another,
we developed a daily routine. We loved to begin each morning with a steaming hot cup of coffee that we shared over our

cozy cockpit table. We enjoyed sitting in silence in the warm sun looking over the water watching fishermen in their *pangas* come and go from the nearby village with their catch of the day. Often you could hear mariachi music in the background blaring from one of the fishermen's boom boxes, or smell the aroma of succulent meat roasting over an outdoor fire. Sometimes a few fishermen would wade waist-deep into the water with their nets. It was true artistry the way they were able to twirl the nets above their heads and get them to spread out and land in a perfect circle before them.

It would have been easy to sit for hours and take in all the smells, sights, and sounds. But shortly after breakfast, Marshall would ask, "Are you ready to go?"

I would answer, "Sure," grab my snorkel gear and spear, and off we would go in the dinghy looking for another new reef to explore.

Even though we spent countless hours snorkeling every nook, cranny, and cave we could find, I always felt a little anxiety just before I put my face in the water and saw what lay beneath us. I didn't know quite what I expected to find, but I always wondered how big or what kind of fish we would run into. We hadn't seen any sharks yet; I was thankful for that.

Because of the intense sun and likelihood of jellyfish in the water we always donned our thin Lycra suits with gloves, hood, and socks. At times the water resembled tapioca pudding, the jellyfish or what we called aqua-mollies were so thick. The Lycra suits worked as a barrier between us and their stings and made snorkeling possible when they were present.

I couldn't get enough of the visual feasts the reefs held. It was like being in an underwater fairyland watching the animated parades of different species, each trying to outdo the other in color and grandeur. I watched them for hours on the stages created by Mother Nature, swimming in and out amongst the crevices of abundant coral and underwater greenery presenting a continuous show of incredible beauty: The exquisite turquoise parrotfish nibbling on coral or whatever he was gathering with his parrot-like front teeth; the colorful and feisty wrasses; or the strange coronet fish, with their long tube-like bodies, hanging as if suspended from an invisible wire. The show was endless, the variety of fish equally so. It was almost hypnotic once I submerged my head below the surface—lunchtime always arrived before I was ready to return to *Clambake*.

It seemed that when we weren't in the water snorkeling, the majority of the day was devoted to the basic existence of life: Finding a fish for dinner, making a dinghy run to the local village for fresh produce, repairing a generator, fixing a new electrical problem, or oftentimes just exploring and mingling with locals, learning as much about their customs and culture as possible.

Fishing took on a new meaning. No longer strictly for pleasure, it was our means of obtaining food for the day. Marshall became very adept with his pneumatic air gun, but it took me a little practice to become proficient with my Hawaiian sling. I would float silently above the surface watching for a fish that I thought I might be able to spear. Once I found my prey, I would wait for the right moment to release the taut rubber band. My arm would quiver from the strain, and finally I would just have to let the arrow spring forward. It always surprised me when I got a fish. Timing was critical; it often took many shots before I could claim success.

Our time in Baja was incredible, but it was the encounters with people that I will remember forever. They seemed to be frozen in time, with basic priorities devoted to survival. They were sincerely warm, happy, and generous with what little they had to share and always had time to help someone in trouble or in need.

Many times I wondered what might have been the outcome if the exact same set of a couple of circumstances had happened in the U.S.A. instead of Mexico. The first incident involved a medical doctor. One day after returning to our boat from a snorkeling session, I was overcome with a sharp, shooting pain radiating across my back. My first thought was that a jellyfish had stung me while we were snorkeling.

"Marshall, could you take a look at my back? It hurts like crazy. It feels like something stung me."

He examined my back carefully. "Well, there is a suspicious red rash in this one area. Do you think we should try and find a doctor?"

"No, it's probably nothing. Let's wait and see how it feels by tomorrow."

The knifelike pain persisted for several days without relief, and I began to think perhaps I had pulled a muscle or possibly had some vertebrae out of alignment. Marshall tried everything, including a massage with Ben Gay and holding me by my feet from the top of the companionway stairs, but nothing seemed to alleviate the pain.

We finally resorted to looking for a doctor in the small town of Loreto. We found a medical clinic in a plain building at the edge of town. We entered and took a seat among a half-dozen locals in the waiting room. The room was small, with about a dozen uncomfortable metal chairs around the perimeter. There were no pictures on the walls and no tables with magazines. There was no visible sign of a secretary.

We waited in silence for about five minutes, when suddenly the doctor appeared in the waiting room and motioned us to follow him. I pointed to the others waiting ahead of us, but he insisted we follow him into another room.

The room he took us into was clean but small with minimal equipment. The doctor was pleasant but spoke limited

English, and with my minimal Spanish vocabulary it was difficult to communicate. I knew the words for back and pain and pointed to the spot that hurt. He examined the area, and from his expression and mannerism, I knew he knew exactly what the problem was.

In his limited English he indicated he was going to get a medical book and would return in about 10 minutes. We thought he told us he was going *home* to get the book. We heard the word *casa*, although we weren't positive that we understood correctly.

Sure enough, in about 10 minutes he was back with a medical book in English opened to a section on shingles. I had them. Maybe boating was more stressful than I had realized, or maybe it was the daily unexpected adventures living with Marshall.

In his limited English the doctor explained that in the U.S., most physicians prescribed cortisone as treatment. He was going to prescribe a series of shots that consisted mainly of high doses of various B vitamins. He explained that although the cortisone treatment alleviated the pain quickly, the shingles would linger. He continued to explain that I would not receive immediate relief with the B shots, but they would help make the shingles go away.

Amazingly, he was right.

The experience astounded me. First, it surprised me that a doctor would see a foreigner before his own people. Next, it astonished me that he would leave a waiting room full of patients and go home in the middle of the day to get a medical book so that I, the patient, could fully understand my problem. After that, I was astounded that the remedy in this third-world country appeared to be more effective than what was being administered n the U.S. The final surprise was his charge for the visit, a mere $17.

Before we left the office, the doctor wrote a prescription

for five vials that I was to pick up at the local pharmacy; he wanted Marshall to administer the shots. Marshall was excited about this. I wasn't. Marshall was mentally envisioning playing Pin The Tail On The Donkey on my derriere.

I quickly gave a radio call to my friend, Dorothy, a retired nurse, and asked for her assistance. She rescued me when she graciously accepted the task. By the fifth day of shots, my pain and most of the evidence of the shingles seemed to have disappeared. I still marvel at how I was treated by the doctor and can't even begin to imagine what would happen at home if the situation had occurred there.

Another memorable experience involved two of our close friends, Fred and Sidonia, whom we met while traveling down the coast of Baja. We had arranged a side outing to see the whales at the saltwater lagoons at Lopez Mateo, a huge calving area, where many gray whale moms and their babies can be seen cruising the estuaries during the month of February. We had rented a minivan for the three-day excursion and did most of the packing the day before we left. Ice chests and camping gear for the four of us were stuffed into every nook and cranny, and our rubber dinghy was tied to the roof rack.

Standing back and surveying our chariot, Sidonia laughingly remarked, "Kind of looks like Ma and Pa Kettle's, doesn't it?"

"It sure does. I just hope it gets us there and back," I replied.

We left early the following morning, rear fender dragging from the load, anticipating arriving at our destination in about three and a half hours. After three hours of driving, we were patting ourselves on the backs that everything was going so well.

Marshall was at the wheel and after looking at the time said, "Well, according to our estimate, we should be arriving at our destination in about half an hour."

Fred, who was following on his roughly drawn map, agreed. "I would say you are right on, looking at the distance left to go."

Following Fred's cryptic directions, we turned off the main highway onto an unmarked dirt road that led toward the ocean and the little village of Lopez Mateo. A short distance from the highway we reached a Y.

"What do you think, right or left?" asked Marshall.

Of course there were no signs. Fred frowned and answered, "My best guess is that the ocean should be off to our left."

"Seems logical," Marshall agreed.

In a few more minutes we came to another Y.

Marshall asked skeptically, "What do ya' think, left again?"

"I'd go left," Fred responded.

Within the next half hour we passed at least another dozen Ys.

"Get out the quarter, Fred, and flip a coin. Heads, left; tails, right," Marshall joked.

We forded small creeks, traversed cow pastures, and passed through gates. The road kept getting narrower. Finally we saw a farmer driving a tractor. With hand signs and some Spanish we were able to explain that we were trying to find the estuaries at Lopez Mateo. Unbelievably, he assured us we were going the right way.

Armed with directions that each of us interpreted differently, we arrived at our destination 45 minutes later. We found a spot outside the village with access to the water. We launched the Zodiac, loaded all of our camp gear, and the four of us squeezed in around the gear and set off to find a campsite on the other side of the estuary.

For two amazing days we watched the whales and their babies in total awe. It was mesmerizing, the experience of a lifetime. Early each morning we would cruise the estuaries looking for signs of the whales. When we spotted a group of them, we would turn off the engine and drift silently with the current.

We probably saw no fewer than 50 pairs of mothers and babies; often we were able to drift to within 15 to 20 feet of them. We never felt we were in danger or threatened. The mothers were docile and usually just floated on the surface with baby on their rear flank. We found ourselves whispering, as we would slowly drift as close as Mom would permit. When she felt we were infringing on her space, Mom would submerge slowly, often rolling baby off in the process.

We were doing a quiet drift on the second day when Marshall remarked, "It's amazing that we are able to get so close to the whales and we haven't had any dangerous close encounters."

Within moments, we stumbled upon a sleeping whale. The drift was perfect: We had floated to within one oar's length from his head. We thought we were about ready to drift by when the sleeping giant woke up. I don't know who was more startled, the whale or us. His tail quickly slapped the water, dousing our dinghy and us. The boat rocked back and forth from the wake as the giant submerged into the depths below.

"Oh, shit . . . oh, my God," I said as the dinghy precariously tipped. "We're going over. Marshall, where did the whale go? Do you see him?" I nervously asked.

"No, I don't."

We strained our eyes searching the water for signs of the submerged whale.

Amazingly, Sidonia maintained her calm and when the boat stopped rocking yelled out in excitement, "I got it, I got it, I got the whole thing on video."

The two days flew by and with remorse we packed the campsite and left in the early morning. We started back across the estuary toward our van, chattering the entire time about our adventure.

"Anyone want to make bets all four hubcaps are still there?" Marshall jokingly asked as we approached our van.

"Yeah, you know if this were L.A., they wouldn't last 30 minutes," Fred chuckled.

Little did we realize how differently people think in Baja.

The van was right where we had parked it. Nothing appeared amiss until we went to start the engine. The battery was dead.

"Fred and I will stay here and get things packed. I see a house across the field; maybe you two girls can walk over there and see if anybody has jumper cables," Marshall suggested.

Sidonia and I exchanged glances. "How did we get volunteered to go looking for help?" I asked.

Looking at the small, rundown house across the way, Sidonia sighed. "I don't hold much hope for a rescue there, but I guess our Spanish is better than theirs," she said, pointing her thumb in the direction of our two husbands. "I guess it's logical that the two of us girls go on the rescue mission."

Ten minutes and one-half mile later, we arrived at the little home. It was even more rustic and rundown than it had appeared from the van. A barefoot little girl stood outside watching us as we walked up to the door. A few chickens and a couple of goats ran around in the dirt yard; in front was parked a very old, rusted, pickup truck.

We said "Hola" to the girl and knocked on the open door.

Two young men appeared. In our limited Spanish, and with a lot of pantomime, we explained our predicament. They seemed to understand. They didn't have a jumper cable, but before we realized what was happening they had removed the battery from their truck. One of them put the battery on his shoulder and they took off for our van, a half-mile across the field.

I tried to make conversation as I hurried to catch up to the two young men. Smiling sweetly, I asked, "Tú es hermosa?"

With eyebrows raised and a very strange expression on their faces, they both suddenly turned to look at me.

Sidonia suppressed a laugh and quickly came to my rescue.

She hastily explained, "Mi amigo's español is muy mal. Tú es hermanos?"

They all started to laugh as Sidonia quietly explained to me I had just asked the two young men if they were beautiful instead of brothers.

Embarrassed, I put my hand to my mouth, laughing, and said "Oops."

It wasn't long before we made it back across the field. Because we had no wires to jump-start the engine, the four men worked together to install the battery and get our van running. They then disassembled it and we all hopped into the crowded van, giving the two fellows a ride back to their home.

They wouldn't accept money for their trouble, so we gave them a couple of boxes of cookies we hadn't eaten on the camping trip. It seemed such an insignificant payment for what they had just done for us. Here we were, for the second time, where total strangers were willing to go out of their way to help us. We were learning quickly that the Baja culture and ways were far different from ours in big cities back home.

CHAPTER 7

The Con Artist

THERE WERE SO MANY BEAUTIFUL SPOTS THAT WE FELL IN love with along the Baja. The Bay of Los Gatos just north of La Paz was one of our favorites. It is a beautiful isolated cove surrounded by spectacular high mountains.

The first time *Clambake* rounded the corner and entered the bay, we could see that we were going to be the only boat there. Not long after we had anchored and settled down to relax in our cockpit, a *panga* appeared from out of nowhere, piloted by a lone fisherman wearing bright red swimming shorts. He pulled up alongside our boat and introduced himself as Manuel. He was a young man from a village several bays away and wanted to know if we wanted to buy any fish or lobster. We said sure, we would like some lobster. He told us he would return in about one hour. We assumed he would be bringing the lobster with him.

When he returned about two hours later, he didn't have any lobster or fish. He went into a long explanation of how he would like to take "Marcos" diving. (Marcos was Manuel's version of Marshall in Spanish.) He offered to show Marcos and me where the lobsters were and to teach us how to harvest them. He was friendly and we accepted his gracious offer.

Marshall cleaning the lobster that didn't get away during the adventure with Manuel.

We grabbed our snorkel gear and spears and hopped into Manuel's *panga* and headed out toward a nearby reef. At the last minute, I decided to remain in the anchored *panga* while Marshall and Manuel snorkeled for the lobster.

The two donned their gear, rolled over the side, and paddled away, kicking their fins, moving swiftly and deftly through the water. I could follow what was going on. They would snorkel for a few minutes on top of the water, stop, dive and then resurface. Marshall was carrying the harvesting bag with the lobster, and as time progressed I could see he was definitely swimming slower, so I assumed the load he was carrying was getting heavier.

After about an hour had passed, I watched as they dove under the surface and disappeared from view for a few moments. Suddenly, I saw Marshall's snorkel aiming at the panga; he was swimming like a bat out of hell. I could hear his panting and heavy breathing all the way to the boat. It was obvious that something was amiss. Manuel was following right behind Marshall. When Marshall arrived at the panga, he threw the mesh bag over the side, pulled off his snorkel, and clung to the side.

Manuel was laughing heartily by the time he arrived. Marshall wasn't.

"What's going on?" I questioned.

It took him a minute to catch his breath. "We got three nice sized lobster and one 10-pound cabrillo," Marshall panted.

"Why the urgency to get back to the *panga*? Are you okay?"

"I'm fine now. Manuel speared about a four-foot moray eel and decided he was going to put that in my bag. Enough is enough. I was out of there when I saw that thing wiggling with his mouth wide open and jaws looking like he might enjoy a chunk of my hide."

Manuel and Marshall pulled themselves up over the side and collapsed in the bottom of the *panga*, Manuel still laughing heartily. In the safety of the panga, Marshall began laughing, too. Manuel took us back to our boat and we invited him aboard *Clambake* for a quick *cerveza* before he started back to his village.

Two hours later he was still aboard, telling stories and having one more *cerveza*. He was quite a character and an incredible storyteller. When he told his stories they were in Spanish, but he used what I call Kindergarten Spanish. His sentences were simple, with lots of hand animation. We knew exactly what he was saying.

Our favorite story, and it was quite a yarn he spun, was about his *amigo* who lived in the *montañas*. He was going to be walking all the way to his *casa* to visit Manuel and his family. His *amigo* had no *zapatos* (pointing to our shoes). He was *muy pobre*. Next thing we knew we were down in our locker pulling out shoes and clothes to give to his friend.

By the time Manuel left our boat that afternoon I think he left with half of our possessions. We had given him fishing gear, canned goods, clothes, shoes, and who knows what else. We couldn't help liking the fellow—he was funny and never asked for anything—but he certainly knew what he was doing and had a very effective technique.

As we continued our travels in the sea of Cortez, we ran into quite a few other cruisers who had had similar experiences with Manuel. He probably provisioned the entire village after his charming and friendly performance.

CHAPTER 8

The Final Preparation

WE PROBABLY COULD HAVE RETIRED IN THE SEA OF Cortez, but the dream of Tahiti and the connection to our family in California spurred us on our voyage. I couldn't bear the thought of not being a part of our grandchildren's lives. And as much as we enjoyed the Baja, it still wasn't Tahiti. It was time to head across to mainland Mexico and continue our journey south.

We traveled down the west coast of Mexico, stopping to explore small villages and the larger tourist towns. Our final stop was Puerto Vallarta, where we planned to do last-minute preparations and provisioning before embarking on our 3,000-mile crossing to the South Pacific. One of our last purchases was a 406 EPIRB, which we hung in the companionway next to our life jackets. Our planning was complete.

Marshall and I often discussed the watches and how we were going to handle them. Even though *Clambake* was a great sailing vessel, she was 52 feet, a lot of boat for the two of us to handle on a long journey. It could be exhausting, especially if we got into bad weather.

We discussed taking on a crew person to help with watches and decided it might be a good idea, especially as a safety precaution. The question was who could we ask to help that wouldn't cramp our comfort zone. We didn't want to invite just anybody; the boat could get real small on a 3,000-mile journey. We needed to find someone who had job flexibility and also had sailing knowledge and experience.

One week before our departure, Marshall suggested, "How about Joe as crew?"

"That's a great idea. He's low maintenance and probably could get off work."

"Yeah, that's what I was thinking, and he has mentioned several times to us if we needed help, just give him a call."

"Why don't you call him and see what he says?"

Later that day, Marshall reached Joe and extended the invitation. He jumped at the chance to join us. We had known Joe for years. He would be perfect. He was low key, flexible, a knowledgeable sailor, and like a brother to us. It would make long watches at night a lot easier with one extra person aboard.

Time flew by and before we knew it, it was the day before our scheduled departure. There still was a lot to do. Joe was flying in later that morning and there was some last minute provisioning of fresh produce. We also had planned a small get-together with some other cruisers for later in the evening on our boat. The morning passed quickly, and when I finally poked my head out of the companionway, there was Joe walking down the dock

Joe was about 5-feet 8 inches tall, lean and muscular, with short sandy-blond hair. He had a boyish look that made him appear much younger than his birth certificate revealed. Even as he sauntered down the dock he portrayed energy in motion.

As I watched him approach, a smile crossed my face as I remembered the last time Joe spent time with us on our boat.

We had gone clamming. Knee-deep in muck, digging away for clams, I remember him saying, "Gosh, guys, this is the most fun I've had since I was a kid."

Since he was a kid, I thought to myself. *Joe, you still are.*

He was going to be perfect to help us make the ocean crossing: Flexible, energetic, and always, always enthusiastic and positive.

"Marshall, Joe's here. Come on up and grab his bag, will you?"

"Hi, Joe. It's wonderful to see you. How was your flight? Did you have trouble finding us?"

"The flight was great. Nope, no problem finding you; I just grabbed a cab and told the driver to take me to the marina. No problem finding your boat, either. You have the tallest mast."

"Come on aboard and get settled in. We're so happy you could get the time off to make the trip with us."

Joe greeted me with a hug and then went below to chat with Marshall and get settled.

"I'll throw my things in the cabin, and then is there anything I can do to help?" he asked.

Marshall answered, "Not really. Why don't you take off for a few hours and do some sightseeing while Dee and I finish up our last-minute projects."

"Perfect. I've never been to Puerto Vallarta before. I was hoping to see a little of the area before we take off tomorrow."

Joe left to take in the sights, sounds, and smells of the city while Marshall and I finished our survey of *Clambake*, making sure everything was securely stowed or lashed down for the long crossing. At the last minute Marshall decided to throw our folding mountain bikes that he had previously lashed to the rail into our tented 12-foot dinghy. I stood there with my hands on my hips watching him.

"At least they will have some protection from the saltwater," he assured me as he glanced sheepishly in my direction.

I sighed. I was not happy with his decision and continued to eye him with disapproval.

He persisted, this time with a lot more authority in his voice. "There is no way we will be getting off a perfectly sound 50-foot sailing vessel to get into a 12-foot rubber ducky. The bikes won't be a problem. Trust me."

I continued with my examination of the boat, checking everything along the way, still not entirely comfortable with the thought that our life raft was becoming *cluttered*. I tried to dismiss my uneasiness and rationalized that Marshall probably was right—what unknown destiny could possibly lie ahead of us that would force us to desert *Clambake* and use the life raft? By evening I had forgotten about the incident.

The cruising community is small and very close. Eventually you meet most of the other boaters heading in the same direction, either through potlucks, beach parties, or just meandering around marinas. Later that evening we found ourselves with 19 fellow cruisers squeezed into our aft cockpit drinking margaritas and discussing last-minute preparations for the 3,000-mile journey. It was a bon voyage party for all of us, because all were planning for the same adventure, heading toward the South Pacific.

"We need to organize a net to stay in touch with each other," one of the cruisers called out.

"I'll volunteer for net controller," someone else chimed in. "We don't plan on leaving for another three weeks."

"How about if we set it for 0900," yelled someone else. "Everybody can check in with their lat and long and weather conditions. That way as we transit, we all have a feel for the weather ahead and behind us."

"Yeah, I like that idea," was echoed by several of the others.

Over on the side rail, two women were discussing canning chicken and how many jars of hamburger they already had put up.

One of the other cruisers forward yelled back to Marshall, "Hey, how about a fishing bet?"

"Sounds good. What do you want to bet on?"

Someone else joined in, "How about the biggest fish caught between here and Tahiti?"

They all agreed and rules were set.

One could almost feel in the air an electricity generated from the excitement that flowed amongst us. Everyone was talking; adrenaline ran high with a quasi-nervous anticipation of what unexpected adventures the trip would bring.

We had made lots of new friends in Mexico and the bonds were growing stronger between us. We were the new explorers, the new fleet crossing the Pacific to those enchanting South Pacific Islands and we all shared the excitement and fears of the adventure that lay ahead.

The group broke apart around 10 o'clock. As the last guest left the boat, I felt a twinge of fluttering in my stomach. We were the second boat scheduled to leave; our journey was to start the following day. Little did we realize that our lives would be changed forever in a few short hours.

CHAPTER 9

Night of Terror

MY LAST VISION BEFORE CLAMBAKE SUBMERGED INTO THE black depths of the ocean was of Marshall lying by the mast on his stomach frantically trying to untie the knots.

The next few seconds blurred as we each dealt with *Clambake*'s deck sliding beneath the water and as we found ourselves going with her. It happened so quickly that the magnitude of the problem had not yet sunk in—that our boat had just gone down and we were in the water in the middle of the Pacific, possibly without a life raft.

Marshall tried to untie that extra line, but the half-hitches couldn't be undone with one hand. It took both. He still was holding our three vacuum-packed bags of $5,000 each in his left hand. As he rapidly untied each of the half-hitches, one cruising kitty bag after another slipped through his fingers and was flung into the sea. He watched them drift aimlessly behind with the current. The choice was clear: Our lives or the cruising kitty. It was our gift to the Sea Gods . . . or some lucky fisherman.

By the time Marshall had undone the three half-hitches, he could feel the water coming up over his legs. He knew he had to work quickly. It seemed as if instantly he was floating on the water, holding onto the lines.

As he worked to free the line, he was pulled farther and farther down.

There's got to be an air pocket caught in the bow. This has got to slow up. . . Damn it, it's accelerating!

He had seen all the war movies with the PT boat sticking straight up and guys sitting on it for days, but it didn't happen that way.

The water had enveloped him. Something hard hit him in the face.

Then he felt something soft. The sail was all around him, a watery shroud seemingly determined to draw him to his grave.

He didn't panic. He just kept pushing the sail to the side and clawing upward, but there was always more sail pulling him down with the boat.

Marshall kept trying to reach the surface, but all of a sudden he realized he was out of air.

I can't get up. Shit, this is a problem. I need air.

The thought crossed his mind that he might not be able to get out of this one.

I became entangled in the rigging. The warm water enveloped me. As I was sucked under the surface, my mind went blank. A tug at my leg brought me back to the moment.

I'm caught, something's wrapped around my leg.

The rigging tightened around my leg as *Clambake* pulled me down with her.

No! No! I have no air! My chest is going to explode. I can't get loose.

Just as I was about to relinquish myself to my fate, out of the depths of my mind came a strange, overwhelming determination. I could hear my mother's song: "I can do it. I can do it . . .if I try."

The rope was tightening, but someone seemed to be guiding me through this tonight. Still holding my breath, I doubled over, bringing my leg up under my stomach. With both hands, I methodically worked the rope off my leg.

At first the lines would not surrender their grip and the water was too black to see anything, but slowly I was able to slide the line down my leg and slip it over my foot. Using both arms, I stroked upward and gasped a big breath of air as I hit the surface. I immediately spotted Joe, but I didn't see Marshall.

"Where's Marshall?" I screamed.

"I don't know," he yelled back.

We both began to shout his name. I dove, but it was so dark I couldn't see anything, not even *Clambake*. *Where is he? Where is he? Where is he? This can't be happening. I'm dreaming. I have to be dreaming.*

I heard him before I saw him. With a loud splash and a louder gasp he broke through the surface, totally out of air.

"My God! Thank Heavens," I shouted. "I couldn't find you. I was so scared. Thank God we're all here."

I was so happy to see Marshall in front of me that I didn't even see the dinghy. It took Joe's shouts of "There it is, there it is!" to make us realize our dinghy had come to the surface. And yes, there she was bobbing upside down, looking every bit like a short, fat, rubber angel to my eyes. Somehow, our dinghy had miraculously broken free and had come to the surface just feet from where we were treading water.

There was no question of trying to right the dinghy. The three of us were out of breath, spent with exhaustion, and half in shock from all that had happened. Marshall and Joe climbed on top of its flat gray bottom. I didn't have the strength to pull myself up, so Marshall reached over and pulled me up alongside them.

The first thing we did was inventory our injuries. There was still some ambient light from the freighter, and luckily the moon beamed bright, so we were able to see each other quite clearly.

Joe had blood running down his face from a head wound; he complained of sharp shoulder and chest pains, and we thought possibly he had some broken ribs. He was doubled over in a hunched position, hardly speaking, but had managed to hang onto the EPIRB during the whole crisis.

We thought Marshall had a broken nose, but other than being exhausted, he appeared to be okay.

I had a severe cut on my head that was bleeding profusely. My head was pounding, I could taste blood, and I was shaking uncontrollably. I didn't think I had broken anything. I can remember uttering over and over, "Thank God we're all here, thank God we're all here." *Yes, life is good, we're conscious, we're functioning, and most important, we're all here and all alive.*

Finally our attention turned upward. The freighter was less than two boat-lengths away. She was steaming off into the night as if none of its crew was aware of what had happened. But close enough to read and still clearly illuminated on the freighter's transom were two giant words now tattooed in my mind and my heart: *HANJIN SAVANNAH*.

Our entire life and future had been altered in no more than 90 seconds.

The bow planer of the 700-foot South Korean container ship meeting the starboard stern of *Clambake* caused the initial jolt we felt. The collision took out the underbody of *Clambake's* stern, which caused us to spin completely around. The second harder jolt, occurred when *Clambake* was hit again by the freighter's midship. The ear-piercing screech was the spreaders on our mast sliding down the steel hull of the ship as we ground our way, starboard to starboard, the entire length of this monster. Even though the second collision sounded the worse, it was the initial blow that mortally wounded our *Clambake*.

But what caused the accident or what had just happened were thoughts for later. Here we were sitting on our upside-down life raft approximately 40 miles from shore and 75 miles from Puerto Vallarta. We had been out to sea just 13 hours into a three-week journey. *Clambake* was on her way to the bottom 3,000 feet below us, and the freighter that hit us was steaming off into the distance. The projections for a safe and quick trip that we had discussed when we left Puerto Vallarta just a few hours ago seemed so far in the past. So much for good omens.

Marshall's adrenaline was still running strong; he immediately decided he had to retrieve the survival bag containing our flare gun before we did anything else. Thinking out loud, he murmured, "A container ship moving at 20 knots will be over the horizon in about 15 minutes. They're our best hope of being rescued; we've got to get its attention."

We had a complete survival bag including everything but the kitchen sink secured to the inside of the dinghy. Because we were sitting on the upside-down floor of our dinghy, one of us would have to get into the water and swim up underneath the Zodiac and cut the bag loose. Joe was severely injured, I had no strength, so Marshall decided it needed to be him.

He dove over the side and under the dinghy to locate the bag. My eyes followed his every movement as he sank beneath the surface and disappeared into the darkness out of sight. I sat there holding my breath, staring at the exact spot in the water that I last saw him.

To my relief, within a few seconds he surfaced, holding the survival bag. It contained a VHF radio, compass, survival blankets, flare gun and 20 flares, and some bags of freeze-dried food, one of which was a package of freeze-dried peas. My heart was still beating wildly as I grabbed the bag and he pulled himself back on top of the Zodiac.

"What about the bikes?" My mind suddenly flashed back to the incident just before we left Puerto Vallarta.

"They weren't a problem, precisely as I told you," he responded with a slight smirk on his face.

Just another gift to the sea gods, I thought to myself as I watched other flotsam and debris from *Clambake* drift past us.

Marshall scavenged through the bag and located the radio, solar blankets, and the flare gun. He handed me the radio and the blankets and then loaded the gun and fired off five rounds in quick succession. They lit up the sky behind the freighter.

"They must see it. Hurry," I urged Marshall. "Shoot some more, or they'll be gone."

I unfolded a solar blanket and wrapped it around Joe and myself. Joe hadn't uttered a word since we had gotten onto the dinghy. He still was clutching the EPIRB but his teeth were chattering and he was staring blankly into space. I felt myself starting to shake. Then I saw some cushions float by.

"Shouldn't we be trying to save some of this stuff?" I asked.

Marshall remained focused and flatly responded, "No, we don't have time to worry about cushions now."

He shot five more rounds into the air. We strained our eyes to watch but detected no sign of change in the freighter's direction or speed. While Marshall was shooting off some of the flares, I started to fiddle with the radio. I flipped the Icon's switch on and off several times but got nothing.

"I can't get the radio to work. It must be dead," I moaned.

Marshall glanced over at me, "I guess being waterproof apparently doesn't include being submerged to the depths our dinghy went down."

I started to think that our options were not looking too good. The radio was not working, we were on an upside-down life raft, and the freighter was showing no indication of turning around to rescue to us. I scanned the horizon but saw no other light in sight, only darkness.

It seemed like the minutes passed relentlessly slowly as we

turned our attention back to watching the freighter fade farther and farther into the horizon. The lights were barely visible. Then something looked different to me.

"I think it's turning, do you see that?" I asked. I was shaking harder and my teeth were chattering. I wrapped the blanket tighter around me.

"No, it's not," Marshall insisted.

"Yes, it is. It is! It is! I see the green light on the starboard side. I couldn't see it before. It's got to be turning," I argued.

We sat in silence staring at the freighter in the distance until we were sure.

Finally, Marshall agreed, "I think I see the red and green bow lights, too."

We now knew it had made the turn and was headed back.

"Yes!" I yelled into the dark. "It's coming back to get us."

In order to help the crew pinpoint our position, Marshall sent up another flare. We watched as the ship turned slightly and then headed directly for us.

"They do have our position, don't they?" I asked.

Then I realized that we had to be almost invisible to the naked eye, sitting on the black bottom of our Zodiac just inches off the water, with only the small light from our EPIRB flashing. Surely they could not see that from the freighter.

"Maybe you should fire another flare so they know exactly where we are," I suggested.

Marshall waited a few seconds. Then a concerned frown crossed his forehead. He turned to Joe and me and grimly said, "I don't want to alarm you, but I'm thinking maybe they aren't looking for us in order to pick us up."

"What do you mean?" I asked.

Joe somberly responded for the first time since we got onto the dinghy, "He means maybe they know what's happened and they'd just as soon not have to deal with any survivors."

That thought hadn't even crossed my mind.

"I'll shoot off one more flare, but I'm saving the last three to launch on their deck if necessary. At least we will leave a mark on their ship. I want you both to be prepared to roll off the dinghy and swim for your lives."

I sat there trembling. *How could we out swim a freighter, especially with all of our injuries?* I knew it wasn't possible. We were doomed, after all.

We sat barely breathing, anticipating the worst, watching the enormous black ship slowly maneuver through the water toward us. It seemed to take hours, hours during which to conjure up all sorts of mental images of what was going to happen. Still sitting on the upside-down dinghy with no means of maneuvering, we were entirely at the mercy of the sea and the huge ship headed straight at us. The only thing in our favor was the gentle swell and mild sea. At least we didn't have to worry about our precarious perch on the dinghy's bottom—that was, until we got into the freighter's wake.

I was now shivering uncontrollably, probably some from shock and some from fear. Fear of how badly we were injured and fear of the freighter bearing down on us. Blood still ran down the side of my face and I could taste it in my mouth; my head was still pounding. Both Marshall's face and Joe's oozed blood. I didn't know how badly any of us were injured, and I was scared to death of what the monstrous black freighter heading straight at us was going to do.

When it was only a quarter of a mile away, we were able to see floodlights sweeping the water as they searched for our exact location. At this point it was hard to know if we should send up another flare and reveal ourselves, or sit in the darkness and let them slip by.

Marshall was an optimist. He shot the flare.

CHAPTER 10

The Rescue

THE 700-FOOT-LONG MOUNTAIN ATTEMPTED TO SLIDE UP alongside our 13-foot rubber raft. As the *Savannah* inched its way closer, we could see men scurrying around the deck; we had to trust they were trying to rescue us. They maneuvered to our windward side in order to block the wind and allowed us to drift into them.

The seemingly calm ocean swells hitting the side of the freighter soon became enormous waves that turned the relatively flat sea into a blender set on "whip." With no sides to protect us on the overturned dinghy, it was all we could do to maintain our precarious perch on its bottom.

The crew doused us with their spotlight and threw a monkey's fist in our direction. I had never seen one before and questioned Marshall as to what they were trying to do.

Instead of answering me, he yelled out, "Watch out! Both of you duck. There's a weighted steel ball at the end of that line they're throwing. They normally use those at the docks to throw the lines into the wind. It's obvious they want us to catch it, but they're going to knock one of us out in the process. This isn't going to work."

They were unable to throw the ball far enough for us to grab, and we couldn't see the line because of the blinding light, but we could hear it hit the water some 50 feet away. Still perched on the bottom of the upside-down Zodiac, we were unable to maneuver and were forced to wait until they came up with another idea.

I guess I didn't know what to expect, but it wasn't exactly my idea of how a rescue was supposed to go. I had pictured something like you see in the movies: They would lower a lifeboat into the water, transfer us from our raft into their lifeboat, and then hoist the lifeboat back on deck. The rescuers would swaddle us in blankets and serve a tot of rum. This scenario wasn't in their rescue journal; the crew continued to throw the monkey's fist toward us.

After one more attempt, Marshall said, "One of us is going to get killed if they hit us with that damn thing. Next time they throw it I'm going to swim for it."

"No, you can't," I panicked. "What if you get sucked into the propeller, or get washed up along the hull of the freighter?"

"I don't intend to let that happen," he promised.

"What if we tie the dinghy line around your waist? That way if you get into any trouble, Joe and I can pull you back." Joe sat silently huddled over in a fetal position the entire time we were discussing what to do. We knew he was in a lot of pain and not doing very well.

Marshall finally agreed, and with a line tied around his waist with a bowline knot, he slipped into the water. With half a dozen strong strokes, he retrieved the monkey's fist and line, then swam back and climbed up onto the Zodiac. I let out a big sigh of relief.

The men on deck pulled on the line and brought us toward the hull and toward the stern of the freighter. We bounced off the waves and into the hull, and back again. We gripped the sides of the dinghy, trying to keep from being thrown off. I was sure one of us would fall off and get sucked under the water into the propellers.

Suddenly Marshall called out, "Look over there, where they're shining the spotlight. There's a rope ladder hanging over the side."

"Oh, my God!" I gasped. "You don't think they want us to climb up that flimsy thing, do you? Do you think that's their version of a Jacob's ladder?" I asked the question, already knowing what the answer would be.

When I looked up, I couldn't see the top. This apparently was how we were going to board the enormous ship.

Thoughts were racing through my mind. *They can't really be serious that this is what they expect us to do. Climb up that swinging ladder? Not in your dreams! There is no way I'm going to climb straight up on a dinky rope while swinging back and forth with the motion of the sea and trying to fend off the physical advances of a steel hull. Can't they see that we are injured?*

I began to panic again. "Marshall, I can't do that. You know how I freeze with heights."

He sympathized but gently encouraged me, "You can do it."

Oh, how I hated hearing those words. Immediately my mom's jingle came back to me. I hated that jingle.

"Just climb straight up and don't look down. At this point they aren't offering any other options, so if we want to be rescued, there is no other choice."

After a few more feeble attempts at arguing that I was not going up that ladder, Marshall and Joe finally convinced me that, no, I was not staying and taking my chances on the raft, and yes, I was going to have to climb up that ladder by myself.

Joe gently pulled away the rescue bag I had been clutching in my arms. I took a deep breath and started the ascent.

I was only halfway up when I heard the men at the top yelling and motioning for the next person to begin.

As Joe handed the bag to Marshall, I yelled down to him, "Please save everything you can. It's all we have."

I started to breathe more quickly again as I felt Joe start up the ladder. The motion was changing; now the swings were more erratic, with two of us climbing. I tried to take a deep breath and calm myself. I felt paralyzed, but Joe was quickly catching up to me, so I forced myself to continue. It appeared I had no alternatives.

I continued upward, not looking down again, and before I knew it multiple arms grabbed me as I reached the sixth deck. Still breathless and shaky but anxious to see how Joe and Marshall were doing, I turned to watch for them. Joe followed quickly and now we both were watching Marshall struggle with our only remaining possessions.

Clear thinking as ever, Marshall made a bowline in the long dinghy line, surmising he could carry the line up the ladder and then get some help to haul up the Zodiac. He slung the survival pack over one shoulder and grabbed the EPIRB with his other hand. The EPIRB is a five-pound canister with a yellow foam-like jacket around its midriff. A 20-foot lanyard was neatly tucked into the buoy portion so the EPIRB was floatable and one could still attach it at some distance from the life raft.

Marshall surveyed the EPIRB; he was out of shoulders and needed his hands for the ladder, so he decided to throw the lanyard around his neck, letting the EPIRB canister drape down his back. He secured it by putting the ring at the end of the lanyard between his teeth. Up the ladder he went, looking like an overloaded bellhop.

About halfway up the ladder, unbeknownst to Marshall, the extra 20 feet of line that had been stuffed into the ring buoy around the canister came loose, allowing it to freefall and almost strangle him. As he felt the canister start to fall, he bit down on the ring and prepared himself for the worst. The canister reached the end of the line and he was able to hang onto everything else and to the ladder.

"Hmmm, not as bad as I thought. I'm still here," he murmured to himself.

We watched from above, holding our breath as he saved himself, the EPIRB, and the survival bag with our freeze-dried peas.

All of us now on board, we hugged each other in relief but in anxious anticipation of what was waiting for us here. Suddenly reality hit as we scanned our surroundings and became aware that we were not alone or on familiar territory. Marshall, Joe, and I had just landed in Korea. Had we exchanged one set of dangers for another?

CHAPTER 11

Friends or Enemies?

WE WERE ENVELOPED BY THE CREW AND HUSTLED through a maze of hallways, down several flights of stairs, and into the ship's infirmary. We obviously were the night's entertainment, as it appeared every crewmember had squeezed into this little room to watch. One of the men stepped forward. He looked no different from the rest—he wore no white smock, carried no stethoscope—but he began to inspect our obvious cuts.

"Does anyone speak English?" I asked, flashing a smile.

Silence . . . then they all seemed to be talking at once, but not one word was understandable.

What language is this? I wondered. I wasn't sure. We would need to brush up on our charades if we were going to communicate at all.

Our medical man covered our head gashes with Liquid Stitch and gave us antibiotics (at least we hoped it was antibiotics we were swallowing). Someone arrived with a mattress and some blankets, and then everyone quickly disappeared. We assumed this was their infirmary. There was one single sterile-looking bed already in the room, and now that another mattress had been delivered, it appeared that this was where we were going to sleep. Our clothes were still wet, but we hardly noticed. We were so exhausted from the ordeal that we crawled into bed without much conversation.

Joe took the single bed. Marshall and I slept on the floor on the double mattress. As I lay there on the mattress looking over at Marshall, I saw a knight in shining armor.

Although I thanked God for giving us another chance at life and was very grateful we were alive, it was not a peaceful sleep. Visions of *Clambake* and the last eight hours twisted in and out of my dreams.

The ship's whistle startled me awake in the morning. A shudder of pain surged throughout my body and brought the reality of last night quickly back to mind. My clothes, still damp from the saltwater, felt sticky against my skin; my body felt as though it had been through World War III. I glanced at Marshall to see if he was still asleep. He was lying there staring at the small white ceiling.

When he saw my eyes flutter open, he sat up and lovingly looked down at me. He forced a grin and facetiously said, "You look cute."

"Good morning to you, too." I sleepily responded. "Where are we? Is Joe awake?"

"Yeah, I'm awake," answered Joe.

"We need to get out of these wet clothes," I muttered to Marshall.

We had arrived on the *Savannah* pretty much like two Adams and an Eve. The guys were wearing only swimming trunks; I was in a tank top and shorts. We had no shoes, no passports, and no money. Except for the clothes on our back and the survival bag with our flare gun, EPIRB, and the freeze-dried peas, we had lost everything.

As we were discussing how we were going to dry our clothes, we were startled by a knock on the door. A young man appeared, carrying dry clothes. He introduced himself as Kim. Kim spoke a little English. He told us he was the first deck officer and would be in charge of helping us. What a relief to have someone we could communicate with—sort of. He handed me a navy sweat suit with the ship's name embroidered on the pocket. Joe got handed a pair of the standard-issue work clothes: Green pants and shirt.

And then there was Marshall. He was about twice the girth of most of the men we had seen on the ship. His thigh measurement probably would equate to their waist measurements. I could see this was a real challenge for Kim.

"Here, try this," he gestured. Hmmm, the garment couldn't even fit over one arm.

Kim ran back and forth several times, obviously confiscating every article of clothing that looked l-a-r-g-e from every crewmember he could find.

Finally, he appeared at the door, all smiles and holding a lovely pair of baby-blue silk pajamas—from the captain, no less! Suppressing a smile, Joe and I admired Marshall's new attire. When Kim left the room, we couldn't contain ourselves and broke into huge grins.

"Boy, will they love him in San Francisco when we return," quipped Joe.

We were escorted to the showers and cautioned against getting our hair wet because of the Liquid Stitch holding our skin together. I spotted a mirror. Aaaaack! I cringed as l looked at my reflection and promised myself that I wouldn't make fun of Marshall in his baby-blue kimono anymore. My hair looked like the plumage of some strange bird, and it appeared I was growing a horn out of the side of my head from all the Liquid Stitch they had applied.

The shower felt like heaven. I let the water run long and hot over my bruised body. Suddenly my emotions let loose and

I found myself crying uncontrollably. I was glad there was no one around to hear.

After the showers, we met at the infirmary to find three pairs of sandals neatly lined up for us. We looked at each other's feet as we slipped them on. My sandals were fine, and Joe's almost fit. Again, poor Marshall was short-changed. The rubber thongs were so short they came only to his instep; it was hard to keep them on his feet when he walked.

Kim reappeared and we were ushered to the dining room. We were assigned our own table in the crew's section, where we sat down to a most unusual breakfast. The cook was used to cooking for hungry seamen, so our plates were heaped high with food. There was a mountain-high pile of rice seasoned with kim chee with a fried egg in the center. Seaweed replaced toast. We thought we were hungry, but finished after a few bites—and it had nothing to do with the delicious, albeit foreign, menu.

The crew looked on as we picked at our food. The events of the last 12 hours were gnawing at us and, try though we might, and as much as we might need to eat, we had too much on our minds to fill our stomachs.

CHAPTER 12

Communications Restored

A S THE SHIP TOOK ON THE ROLE OF SANCTUARY, HOSPITAL, and cafeteria, our thoughts turned to family and friends. Our cruising friends believed we were merrily sailing on our way to Tahiti and doing just fine, and we thought our family believed we were lost at sea. We had some contacts to make. We needed to get in touch with our cruising friends, but more importantly, we needed to reach our daughter, Sheri. She was the person listed as our contact on the EPIRB. Our distress signal, when activated, was to have pinpointed our position, identified us by name and had given the name and phone number of the person we had specified to call in an emergency. We surmised Sheri would have been notified, and by now, if she had reached everyone, the whole family must be in a state of panic. We waited for the 0900 cruiser's net when we would be able to contact them and allay their fears.

One reason most cruisers have a ham radio on board is to take advantage of the broadcast networks for the cruising community. At 0900 most days, we tuned in to the Chubasco net, where we could hear weather information, talk to other cruisers, and contact people back home. This all happened through volunteer efforts of a net controller and other ham operators acting as relays in varied locations. This particular net originated in Southern California, with relays located in most of the western states.

To contact someone who wasn't ham-equipped, we enlisted the help of one of the volunteers to patch us through, using a phone modem in connection with the radio to place a call. It was an amazing process. Even more amazing was the time (three to four hours every day) these volunteers devoted with no compensation other than the admiration of the people who benefited from their endeavor. Each one was an unsung hero.

Right after breakfast, Marshall talked to Kim about the possibility of using the ship's radio to talk to our family. Kim understood our request and obtained permission from the ship's chief radio engineer.

We reached the radio room a few minutes before 0900. The chief engineer acknowledged us, took the sheet of paper on which Marshall had written down the frequency, and turned to tune in the radio. To our dismay, he seemed to be having a problem with the radio. Before we knew it, he had grabbed a small hammer that was lying on the desk in front of him and lightly tapped the radio twice.

Marshall and I glanced at each other. I silently mouthed to Marshall, "Oh, no; not looking good."

Suddenly there was some static and it appeared the radio was working. I glanced at Marshall again with a sigh of relief. The engineer turned the knob and tuned into our frequency just in time for us to hear the opening of the net. This consisted of a brief description of the net's purpose, followed by the first order of business.

"Is there any emergency traffic?" an officious voice queried.

"This is *Clambake*," Marshall's voice broke the routine silence.

After being recognized, he proceeded to address our Tahiti-bound friends, "Well guys, I think you might as well give up any idea of winning the biggest fish contest, cause I can't imagine anyone outdoing the 700-foot one we landed on our transom last night!"

A barrage of questions followed his explanation of our last eight hours. "When and where are you getting off? Are any of you badly injured? What is the name of the freighter you are on and what nationality is it? What can we do to help?"

Marshall, Joe, and I exchanged glances as we realized we had no answers to a lot of their questions.

While Marshall was handling the microphone and trying to answer what questions he could, I sauntered over to an eight-foot map of the world on the back wall in the radio room. I indicated our approximate position to the chief engineer, shrugged my shoulders, and slid my finger in different directions along the map, hoping he would realize I was trying to ask him, "Where are we going?"

He walked over to the map and drew his finger along the Central American coast, through the Panama Canal, through the Caribbean, and up the eastern coast of America to Savannah, Georgia. Ahh, *Hanjin Savannah*, the ship's name! Now it made sense.

Pointing at Marshall, Joe, and myself, and by indicating the same path, I questioned, "Are we going with you?'

"Yes," he confirmed by nodding.

"Oh my!" Pointing at the calendar and holding up different increments of fingers, I asked, "How many days?"

Eight fingers was the response.

My, oh my! I thought. At that moment Marshall passed the radio to me to relay this information to our cruising friends. I leaned toward the speaker. "We've always wanted to go through the Panama Canal, and now it appears we are definitely going to do it."

It was time now to broach our main concern of getting in touch with our daughter. Before anyone else could respond, the net controller jumped in.

"I need to know if this is a North or South Korean freighter?"

I looked at Marshall and Joe, who shrugged their shoulders. "We don't know," I replied.

"Well, we don't have reciprocal radio privileges with North Korea. If we continue contact with you and the ship is in fact from North Korea we could possibly lose our license," he informed us.

This came as a shock and I was immediately on the verge of tears. I didn't know what to say. This was our only means of communication, and I couldn't stand the thought of not speaking to our family for eight more days.

"All I want to do is get in touch with our family and let them know we are all okay. I certainly don't want to be the cause of anyone losing his radio license," I pleaded.

After a few minutes of silence, our Portland contact, Ralph, came back "As far as I'm concerned, this is an emergency and I don't care where the ship is from. These folks need help, and I'm going to make sure they get it."

A cruiser in Puerto Vallarta jumped in with an offer to contact Sheri by phone and let her know we had been rescued and were safe. Ralph offered his services to patch Sheri through to us that afternoon on the Mañana net. Oh, what a relief to have this kind of support when we were feeling so helpless.

After we cleared the frequency, we questioned Kim about our passenger status. He explained that no stops would be made on our account. We were safe and no one was in need of emergency medical treatment, so the ship's only obligation was for the crew to deliver us to its next port of call, which was Savannah, Georgia.

How foolish of us to have hoped for anything else.

Our next question was a little harder to ask. "Is the *Hanjin Savannah* a North or South Korean ship?"

The radio engineer, who hadn't given any indication he spoke or understood English, and Kim, answered in unison. "We're a South Korean ship."

Marshall, Joe, and I exchanged glances and I exhaled a sigh of relief. *At least we won't have to worry about politics as a subplot to this melodrama,* I mistakenly thought.

As we left the radio room we decided to walk around the 1,400-foot block, the perimeter of the freighter. Because the upper-deck passage was narrow, we started off in single file. I was the leader of the pack strutting a soldier's march, lifting my legs and swinging my arms as I stretched my sore muscles. Joe followed at a pretty good gait but because of his broken ribs took on a Groucho Marx slouch with arms pasted to his side. Marshall brought up the rear in his baby-blue kimono doing the Savannah shuffle. He couldn't raise his feet so he resembled an ice skater skimming across the metal decks in order to keep those ill-fitting sandals on. The crew couldn't take their eyes off of us as we paraded around.

Our excursion soon turned educational. First we noticed that the radar antenna on top of the pilothouse wasn't spinning, which meant the radar wasn't on. A radar antenna in operation turns as it scans the horizon. This unit was still. We had wanted to ask if the radar was on at the time of the accident, but we didn't know how, or to whom to pose the question. Staring at the radar now, we couldn't determine if it was off because it was daylight and they were keeping a people watch, or if perhaps the radar was out of commission and also hadn't been working the night before.

We reached the bow of the freighter and saw no crew in sight. Marshall decided to take advantage of the moment. He leaned over the starboard rail as far as he could and told Joe to hold onto his feet. He confirmed his hunch that the spreaders from *Clambake's* mast had left visible scars on the ship's side.

"They definitely are there, as well as some huge scratches on the bow planer, and it is obvious they were from us," he exclaimed as Joe pulled him back to safety and we continued our walk.

The *Hanjin Savannah* was a marvel of a modern ship. It had the latest technology, and its efficient crew maintained it meticulously. Of the 17 men on board, three were full-time painters who didn't allow one inch of rust to be found anywhere on the massive hull.

"Well, they're going to have a hard time claiming that they weren't the ship that ran over us. Not with those scrapes on the hull," Marshall remarked.

"What are you saying?" I questioned. "How could they possibly think there was any other reason we were floating around in the open ocean on an overturned dinghy at one o'clock in the morning?"

"Of course it sounds crazy to us," Marshall said, "but I got the distinct impression last night from the crew that they didn't know how we ended up out there. And I might be wrong, but one of the older men, maybe the captain, was shaking his head "no" when I explained we'd been run down by the *Savannah*. It's so hard to know if they understand more of what we are saying than they let on, or if we are just guessing at what the other is saying."

Joe nodded in agreement. "I don't think they honestly had any idea that they'd run over us. Maybe they think we developed a major leak and the boat just sank out from under us."

"Maybe, but they couldn't possibly believe we were run down by anyone else," I chimed in. "There wasn't another boat in the area, and it was perfectly clear last night."

"As soon as we dock in Savannah we have to get photos of the starboard side," Marshall announced. "I don't think it will be difficult for a marine surveyor to prove that the distance between the two spreaders on our mast is identical to the distance between the two 20-foot-long scratches along their hull. From what I could see just now, those are the only marks on the hull. That's pretty irrefutable evidence we were rammed."

We didn't have much time to enjoy our masterful bit of detective work before we encountered three men busily scraping away every speck of rust and repainting the ship to perfection. We looked at each other in silent recognition that our proof wouldn't last 15 minutes after reaching the first dock. Our proof may have been irrefutable, but it wasn't everlasting.

"Our kingdom for a camera," I sighed.

Marshall somberly replied, "I don't think we can even buy a roll of film with what's left of our kingdom."

The sanding and painting stopped and the men excused their way around us, heading down the deck and motioning for us to follow. *Oh, oh*, I thought. *What have we done now? Have we committed a* faux pas *or gone somewhere we shouldn't have? Maybe someone saw Marshall hanging over the rail and was concerned about what we were doing.*

It was so darn frustrating not knowing the language or the rules. We figured we were headed for some sort of questioning or reprimand, but to our surprise ended up at the cafeteria. We passed by one small dining room we hadn't noticed before—it apparently was only for officers. We followed the three men into the larger mess hall for the crew. We may have been guests, but we were neither official nor honored, and our status was clear. We felt like the new kid at school and could feel the constant stares of our classmates, but there was no hazing and no snubbing. They treated us with gracious curiosity.

We took our place at our assigned table and then, taking our cue from those around us, joined the cafeteria line to make our selections. This was the main meal of the day and it was abundant. Big bowls of soup again, rice, vegetables, and of course, kim chee. And what was this? It looked like raw chicken. Now, we were familiar with raw fish, but raw chicken? I was sure the FDA wouldn't approve!

Noticing our dilemma, the man behind me tapped me on the shoulder and pointed to the wok on the table. Ahh, now I understood. A wok on every table certainly solved the old problem of not getting food cooked the way you like it. Everyone did his own cooking. I was going to like this. We sat down at our table, separated from the rest, and observed our new hosts as they showed us in exaggerated pantomime the finer points of wok cooking. Smiles and nodding were finally displaced by the desire to eat. We did our best to make a dent in the huge portions, but it was too much for our nervous stomachs and worried minds. Again, we left food behind.

Kim met us as we were leaving the dining room and motioned for us to follow him to our new quarters. As we arrived in an upper hallway, he pointed to Marshall and me and gestured toward the one room.

"You two go to owner's stateroom," he ordered in his broken English. "It is big, two rooms. Very nice. Has own bath. Owner only here one time on our ship. No one else stay here. Very nice, you like?"

As I peeked into the room, I thought, *I'm in heaven*. It was a spacious two-room suite with a nice sitting area complete with a television, VCR, and a huge bathtub to soak! Meanwhile, Joe was shown to a nice room across the hall.

In the main hallway we found a picture gallery of the ship's officers. We began to match faces with names and ranks. Kim was the equivalent of a first-deck officer, as we already had surmised.

The captain was confirmed as the man we thought. He had yet to speak directly to us. Through his demeanor alone we understood we could not be the ones to initiate a conversation with him.

Before I had a chance to enjoy my new surroundings, I received an invitation to meet with the chef. As I headed toward the galley I pictured myself standing next to this master, learning the secrets of Korean cooking. My time would be well spent, because I loved to cook and Marshall loved to eat. But, as was becoming a constant occurrence, what I envisioned and what I would experience were not remotely related.

I entered the spotless, stainless steel kitchen and found the chef standing in front of the stove stirring a huge pot. Something smelled wonderful. He acknowledged me with a grunt and then hustled over to a cupboard and pulled out a loaf of plain white generic bread. He then opened a container of processed cheese and motioned me to go over to the stove. Not having a clue as to what was going on, I stood there politely smiling. He stared at me and then flailed his arms motioning to the ingredients and the stove.

Oh my God, he wanted me to cook an American grilled cheese sandwich.

He apparently thought that because we were not cleaning our plates, we didn't like his cooking, or that we didn't like Korean food. *Oh no,* I thought, *how am I ever going to let him know that we don't want Wonder Bread and cheese paste when we can have the delicious meals he provides?* Now I was really nervous. *How do I get my point across?*

I saw and smelled the pots simmering on the stove and slowly slid over to them. I rubbed my stomach, trying to show him that I was enjoying the wonderful aromas. Then I captured the steam in my hands and brought it to my nose while smiling and humming like a complete idiot. Then I pointed at my eyes, then to him, then to the stove, hoping he would understand that I wanted to watch him.

All I heard was a "Harrumph" as he turned his back on me to tend to his pots. I stood by the wall and watched as he worked in obvious agitation. He gave me quick sideways glances and shook his head in disapproval until I finally bowed my way backward out of the kitchen, where I obviously was unable to take the heat.

"Back so soon?" Marshall asked.

"Yes, and I've just failed Cooking 101 and Foreign Relations 101 simultaneously," I replied.

"Oh no, you didn't piss off the cook, did you?" Marshall was immediately concerned about his next meal.

"I certainly did, and we may be fasting for the rest of this trip," I told him as I relayed the rest of what had just happened.

"Oh great, and just when I was really beginning to like kim chee and dried seaweed!" my best friend and husband teased as he tried to cheer me up.

That afternoon we tried to explain to Kim what had happened so he could explain to the cook. That evening we were relieved when we again were accepted into the dining room. We were beginning to form silent but animated friendships with the crew. Relations between the chef and me, however, were irreparably strained; I continued to wither under his gaze each time we met.

It soon was time for the three of us to head back to the radio room for our prearranged phone patch with Sheri. As traumatic as the last 24 hours had been for us, I could only imagine the anguish the family had been going through since receiving word from the Coast Guard that our EPIRB had been activated. I suspected they had imagined the worst, while obviously hoping for the best. Evie, the cruiser from Puerto Vallarta, told us as soon as the net began that she had called Sheri via phone and explained the situation to her as best she could.

"Oh, Mom, I can't believe what happened," were Sheri's first words to us.

"Yes, and it's pretty hard for us to believe, too," I told her. "I'm so sorry you had to worry for so long before you could find out what happened."

And then she told us, "You know what, Mom? I never got a call from anybody about anything until Evie called this morning."

Good God, how could that be, Marshall and I silently communicated with a look.

"Well, honey, I can't imagine what happened that you weren't contacted by the Coast Guard, but I'm glad you didn't have to worry. All that matters now is that we're OK and we'll be back in the States in eight days."

Sheri replied, "I've called Grandma and Grandpa in Pennsylvania; they were sitting in the living room reading the newspaper when I called. They said they had talked to you through a ham radio patch just before you left Puerto Vallarta and were shocked to hear about your accident. They called me back this morning. You know them. They have nothing to do but think about things like this, so they came up with a plan. They said they are going to get in touch with somebody, I can't remember who, but it was someone in government, I think a senator, whom they thought would be able to offer some kind of help to get you off the ship sooner and be able to help make arrangements to fly you home."

"Doesn't that just sound like them?" I asked her. "They can't sit and wait, but want to do something to help—and knowing them, they will find somebody who can do it. Although I can't imagine anything can be done for us until we reach Georgia."

"Now, Mom," Sheri demanded, "I want you to be honest with me. How badly are you hurt? And did they do anything to take care of your injuries?"

I assured her, "Our injuries were minor, and yes, they are treating us and taking good care of us. They have been very congenial, so please don't worry; tell the rest of the family not to, either."

I could tell by the catch in her voice that she wasn't convinced. To be honest, I didn't blame her lack of belief. I still was in awe how three people could possibly survive being run over by a freighter, lose their boat, and escape with no more than a couple of broken ribs and a few cuts and bruises.

"They told us we'll be going through the Panama Canal with them and won't be able to get off the ship until we arrive in Georgia," I explained to her. "I really don't want you to worry; we really all are fine and are being treated very well."

"Okay, Mom. Is there anything we can do on this end?" she asked.

"The only thing would be to let everyone know we are okay and maybe call the insurance company for us and make them aware of what happened. I will contact them as soon as we reach the States. I will try and stay in touch with you as I know more information, but I don't know how often we can use the radio."

We finally said goodbye. I signed off just in time, because I was no longer able to hold back the flood of tears. I felt terrible about the trouble and worry we had to be causing the family back home, but I was grateful we had been given another chance at life and that I soon would be able to see them again. The accident reminded me one more time how fragile life is, and that family and friends are all that matter.

As I turned the microphone back to the radio engineer, Marshall blurted out, "What the hell happened with the EPIRB?" All three of us stood there thinking about that for a second.

"Joe, you activated it right away, and it was still operating until well after we got on board the ship. I didn't remember to shut it off until after they had finished patching Dee up in the infirmary. I don't know exactly how long we had it on, but it had to be long enough for the signal to have been received. It just doesn't make any sense."

"No, it doesn't," Joe agreed. "From what I remember of how these things work, the signal is picked up when a satellite passes over, but I'm not sure how often that happens."

I cringed at the thought that if we hadn't been picked up by the *Savannah*, we might not ever have been rescued.

"Here's something else we need to investigate when we get back," Marshall sighed. "Thank goodness we still have it with us. It shouldn't be too difficult to find out what happened."

As we were ready to leave the radio room, the operator told us we had another call. It was from the U.S. Coast Guard. Marshall took over on the radio.

It was the usual questions the Coast Guard asks when filling out an accident report: Our names, how many people on board, ages, addresses, the size and color of the vessel, whether we were wearing life jackets. The officer wanted to hear our version of the accident as best we could remember, and on and on and on.

"Try and sit down with the captain and go over the accident as you both see it. Your time on the ship is the only chance you will have to find out what the captain and the crew really know," the Coast Guard officer urged Marshall.

That was definitely good advice, although more difficult to carry out than one might think. The language barrier was only part of the problem; the captain still was being very elusive. He ostentatiously kept his distance, making it impossible to approach him.

That night in our stateroom the three of us, with no other entertainment available, dove into a game of tic-tac-toe. We left the stateroom door open and invited Kim in when he passed by.

We showed him how to play the game and engaged him in what little conversation we could.

Finally, Marshall felt he had an opportunity to broach some of the questions we had been bouncing around among the three of us. He drew a diagram of how he thought the accident occurred and then turned the pencil over to Kim. Kim shrugged his shoulders and laid his hands to one side of his face, indicating sleep.

"I think he's saying he was asleep at the time," said Marshall.

He turned back to Kim. "How many people were on the bridge?" he asked by drawing a picture and holding up fingers.

One finger was the reply. Kim haltingly expressed his deep pride that theirs was such a sophisticated ship that 16 men could sleep and only one man was needed at the helm.

"What about radar?" Marshall queried.

"No screen," Kim replied. What did that mean? That the screen wasn't working or that we didn't show up on their screen? It was too complicated a thought to express in pantomime or the simple language we could use with each other, so it went unanswered.

Marshall tried one last question. "Did your ship turn around to come back and rescue us?"

Although we were 99 percent sure there was no other boat in the area that could possibly have hit us and then gone off into the night, a lot had happened in a very short time, and for some of that time we were under water and in shock. We needed to verify the true course of the *Savannah*. We needed to know that she was the same ship we saw from our cockpit, and then later the same ship we saw turn around and ultimately rescue us. The fact that she did not come from the opposite direction was critical. We sat there waiting in anxious anticipation for Kim's answer.

We breathed a sigh of relief as Kim sketched a picture of their boat on a course of 125 true magnetic doing a U-turn. They had been on the Great Circle Route from Puson, Korea, when we intersected paths.

"Yes," he admitted, "we altered course and turned around when the ship's alarm sounded."

Marshall and I talked long into the night about the unanswered questions, such as: (1) who was at the helm on the freighter? (2) Was the radar working? (3) If it was, why didn't they see us? (4) Will the captain ever allow us to talk to him? (5) Why didn't Sheri get a call when the EPIRB signal was received?

As I rolled over in bed to finally get some sleep, I thought, *Well, at least we have seven more days to get some of these questions answered.*

As the days on the freighter clicked by, we developed a little daily routine. It became our habit to walk around the entire freighter on the outer upper deck after each meal. This provided us with a little exercise and an innocent opportunity to regularly monitor whether or not the radar was on and working. We also were able to pick up bits of information here and there about the Hanjin Shipping Co., which we found out later was one of the largest companies in Korea.

After our walk, we always returned to our stateroom, and within minutes a young gentleman would appear to diligently check our wounds and apply more Liquid Stitch. We were growing little mountains of plastic over our wounds with each application.

Joe and I would look at each other and utter an, "Oh well, glad no else can see us like this."

The greater part of each day was spent talking and taking notes about all we could remember of the sequence of events. Although we generally were alone, we had the feeling we never were out of the crew's sight.

Wednesday evening after dinner and our stroll around the ship, we returned to our cabin to play a little Hangman and await Kim's nightly arrival. But instead of Kim arriving this evening, a young gentleman knocked on our door and asked permission to join us. He spoke some English and told us he was just out of officer's school and this was his first assignment. He explained that students were required to learn English in school, but they always were so concerned with the grammar and passing the tests, they never spoke it. He was eager to practice on us. He did quite well. He was curious about our yacht and our trip and had many questions.

After we answered everything we could, we gently approached the subject of the accident and started to draw on a sheet of paper what we thought had happened. He was just about to draw his version of it when the captain walked by our door and nodded to him. He politely excused himself and we never saw him again. Later that evening we matched his picture on the wall with a name and jotted it down in our notes.

Two months after returning home, our attorney sent us copies of several depositions the Coast Guard had taken from the crew when the ship arrived at Savannah. One of the depositions was from the man who was on watch the night of the accident. We believe the young man who visited us in our room was that man on watch that fateful night, and we often wonder what happened to him—if he lost his job because of the accident. He was such a pleasant and bright young man.

One other notable event occurred while we were on the ship. They allowed us to roam freely aboard the huge freighter, with the exception of the pilothouse. We poked around in their lounges and found all sorts of interesting brochures and magazines on the Hanjin Co. When no one was around, I copied the names of the company executives, including the name of the CEO. More urgently than anything else, however, we wanted to see the pilothouse before we departed the ship, to determine if the *Savannah's* radar was working. When we questioned Kim as to whether they saw us on radar, his answer was always the same: "We had no screen."

Every day we asked for a tour of the pilothouse. "Maybe later in the week," he always placated us.

It was beginning to look as if we would never get to see it, and then . . .

We had finished dinner Thursday evening and were leaving the dining room, when Kim approached us in the hallway. Out of the blue he invited us to join him for a tour. Marshall and I looked at each other and couldn't suppress our smiles. Was he inviting us to see the pilothouse?

We jumped at the opportunity to join him, hoping the tour would include the pilothouse. It did and it was very impressive, including the demonstration of its huge and very modern radar, which appeared to be working just fine.

Very interesting, I thought.

The next morning on our daily walk, we noticed the radar dome was spinning for the first time since we had boarded the ship.

"Marshall, do you think they just fixed the radar yesterday and that is why we got the invitation last night to tour the pilothouse?"

"That is the big question, isn't it?" he solemnly replied.

CHAPTER 13

Understanding Our Position

After breakfast on Thursday we were invited to join the captain in his quarters to discuss the accident. Kim led us to the captain's quarters, which turned out to be right next to ours. We had suspected that they were, but never saw the captain enter or leave the room, so we were never able to confirm that belief.

Kim formally introduced us to the captain for the first time. He graciously shook our hands and asked us to be seated in his spacious salon. He made a gesture with his hand indicating he wanted Marshall to begin the conversation.

It was a trying discussion, because the captain didn't speak any English and translations had to be done through Kim, whose English was limited. We all resorted to a lot of drawing.

Marshall started off drawing a picture of the two ships and their approximate courses—the *Savannah*'s heading of approximately 125 degrees magnetic and *Clambake*'s heading of 220 degrees magnetic. He turned the drawing around for the captain, who was sitting directly across from us, to verify. The captain, looking very solemn, nodded his head yes in agreement.

Next Marshall drew a picture with the freighter hitting *Clambake's* stern and then arrows showing how we slid down its starboard side. The captain shook his head "no" and took the paper and drew a picture showing us sliding down his port side. There was a big discussion between Kim and the captain in Korean.

Marshall and I looked at each other in confusion. We knew that definitely wasn't the situation. *Now what do we do?*

I started to explain to Kim, "As *Clambake* was sinking, we saw the *Savannah* on our starboard side and our bow was facing the stern of the—"

The captain interrupted and again spoke to Kim in Korean. Kim said something in return, and turned to us and said, "Do you have any more questions?"

Marshall and I said, "Yes" in unison.

It appeared that the captain was finished and was trying to dismiss us. We had no intention of leaving until we got a few more answers.

I asked Kim if we could please have the name and phone number of someone to contact from the Hanjin Company when we returned to the States. We already had told Kim about our sailboat and all that we had lost. We explained that *Clambake* was our home and that everything that was important to us was on board. I reiterated this again for Kim to explain to the captain.

We waited while Kim translated. It was apparent from his impatient demeanor that the captain was not sympathetic to our material losses. He had Kim relay to us that he would obtain a name and phone number of someone in Hanjin's main office in New York before we left the ship.

We could tell Kim was in a difficult position. He smiled at us sympathetically. He knew we had more questions but obviously was required to comply with the captain's demands.

Marshall turned to Kim and asked, "Can you ask the captain's permission for us to remain on his ship until Savannah, Georgia?" The radio engineer had indicated that we would be staying on the ship until then, but that information had not been confirmed by anyone else.

Again Kim talked to the captain in Korean and gave us his answer. "The captain will talk to Hanjin's head office and let you know later this afternoon."

At this point, Kim rose as if to usher us out. It was obvious that the captain had nothing more to say. Marshall and I stood up and thanked the captain and Kim. We left the room frustrated and with the distinct feeling that the captain did not want to discuss anything else in regard to the accident, possibly to protect his case later on.

We were not sure this meeting gave us any real answers as to what really happened that evening, but at least the captain had a drawing of what *we* believed happened and knew that it definitely involved his ship. The one positive result of the meeting was that we would be receiving a name and a phone number from the captain of a man who worked at the Hanjin office in New York. At least we would have a person to contact to discuss our losses when we arrived home.

There still was one perplexing piece to the puzzle that confused Marshall, Joe, and I. Kim and the captain kept saying *Clambake* had been on their port side. Their pictures indicated this. We saw and knew we were on their *starboard* side. The captain confirmed his heading; we knew our heading. It made sense that we should have been on their port side, but we weren't. How did we end up on his starboard side? Marshall, Joe, and I pondered this question for hours.

"Joe, tell us again exactly what you saw and remember," said Marshall.

"I remember feeling a presence and looking back and the ship was heading straight at us," said Joe repeatedly, decidedly frustrated. "It doesn't make sense to me, either. I tried to turn the wheel as she was bearing down on us, and that is the last I remember about anything until I was on the life raft."

It wasn't until a couple of months later that we learned the answer to this perturbing question. As it turned out, there was nothing any of us aboard *Clambake* could have done to prevent the accident.

Back home in Pennsylvania, Grandma and Grandpa were able to track down someone in the State Department who could help. They first called Senator Arlen Specter's office. His secretary, Ms. Bierman, called the State Department and the Korean Embassy. This started a chain of events.

Ms. Clark of the Korean Embassy called our daughter, Sheri, for information about us and our approximate location at the time of the accident. Next, Ms. Clark contacted the maritime attaché at the Korean Embassy, Mr. Kim. He, in turn, was able to obtain the name and the location of the ship.

This information was passed on to Robert Heaps, head of the Citizens Overseas Emergency Services, a division of the State Department. Grandma and Grandpa ultimately put Heaps in touch with Sheri, and they made arrangements to get us off the ship in Panama. Sheri wired money out of our account to the State Department, which in turn wired it to the Ambassador of Panama.

We had no idea this was going on, so at our morning meeting with the captain, Marshall had asked permission for us to remain on his ship until it arrived in Savannah. We had thought it would be a lot easier to deal with officials in our country than to try to cope in a foreign country without passports or money.

You can imagine our surprise when Kim came to our room Thursday afternoon to announce a call waiting for us from the State Department.

Marshall and I looked at each other in surprise. "Why would the State Department be calling us?" I asked Marshall.

"I have no idea," he responded. "I can understand the Coast Guard possibly calling back, but I can't imagine what the State Department would want."

Marshall and I accompanied Kim to the radio room. On the way, he informed us that the captain had confirmed with Hanjin's head office that we could remain on his ship until it docked in Savannah.

We entered the radio room for the third time since our arrival on the ship. The chief engineer smiled and pointed at the mike hanging by the radio.

Marshall took the mike.

"Hello, Marshall, this is Robert Heaps from the State Department. We have been in contact with your folks and your daughter and have made arrangements for you to get off the ship in Panama in two days."

We glanced at each other in confusion and surprise. "That's great, but just this morning I obtained permission from the captain to stay on the ship until we reach Savannah, and it has been cleared by his head office," Marshall explained.

"That's too bad," said Heaps with disappointment in his voice. "Can you talk to him and change the plans?"

"It's not that easy," Marshall explained. "We have a severe communication problem, plus the captain is very elusive. Also, I'm sure he will have to clear it with his main office again, and I know he won't be pleased about that."

"Well, how about this, Heaps said. Why don't you see what you can work out with the captain, and we will continue with our plans from this end, hoping you can make it work on your end."

Marshall agreed to try, although he knew it was going to be a challenge. Heaps said he would call at 1300 tomorrow to find out what Marshall had been able to accomplish.

We left the radio room discussing how we should approach this. "Obviously we need to talk to Kim first," said Marshall. "This isn't going to be easy to explain, since a lot will have to be done through pictures and pantomime and pointing to maps, and so forth." I agreed.

We were right in our assessment that the captain would not be happy that he had to call the head office again to request a change in plans. His aggravation was very apparent, although we didn't understand one word he was saying to Kim. The hard part to explain was that it was our State Department orchestrating this back home.

We were very impressed with this government agent's efficiency. Exactly at 1300 the following day, Kim came to us to announce Heap's call. The captain had begrudgingly given us permission for the new plan and Marshall relayed our success to the official.

"That's great," Heaps said. "We will finalize the details here and get back to you with all the specifics."

Marshall hung up the phone, turned to me, and said, "It looks like we'll be getting off the ship either tomorrow or the next day in Panama."

Again, the language barrier made it difficult to understand what really was going to take place. As with our rescue, we had drawn a mental picture of how we would disembark the ship. We assumed that because we were transiting the locks, the crew would simply lower or swing out a ramp on which we would be able to walk off the freighter onto land.

One more time, what we envisioned and what was about to happen were as far apart as Tahiti and us. Our exit would be almost as dramatic as our entrance and it would leave a lasting impression of our acquaintance with the *Hanjin Savannah* and its crew.

Saturday morning we arrived in the Bay of Panama and were anchored among numerous other freighters waiting our turn to transit the locks. We had not heard from Heaps, so we assumed we would not be getting off the ship that day.

We had finished our morning walk around the perimeter of the freighter and returned to our room when Kim arrived and announced they wanted us on A deck immediately. He handed Marshall a pair of jeans and golf shirt to replace his baby-blue kimono.

Unsure as to what was happening, Marshall changed into his new wardrobe. We grabbed our sole possession, the survival bag, and followed. Once there, Kim instructed us to remove our sandals and handed me a pair of workmen's gloves. Next thing we knew, Kim pointed toward the exit port and ramp within the sidewall of the ship. He ushered us down the five-foot ramp to our ever-so-familiar Jacob's ladder, the same swinging rope ladder that had welcomed us aboard the freighter on the night of our rescue. He indicated for us to crawl down the six stories of the swinging ladder.

I couldn't believe they were going to dump us in the sea after they had rescued us, patched our wounds, clothed us, and provided us with five days of wonderful meals. I timidly peeked over the rail. To my relief I saw a small skiff bouncing up and down in the roll of the sea. It was waiting just a few feet from the freighter; obviously this was the way we were going to get to shore.

Before starting the descent, I gave Kim a big hug. The captain was stoically standing by his side. I went to shake his hand and give him a thank-you letter the three of us had composed for the crew, but at the last minute I gave him a big hug, also. I detected a slight bit of emotion from him as I stepped back. I knew we would never again see our rescuers and new friends. With tears running down my cheeks, we started our descent.

Now the question was, were we going to be able to jump aboard the bouncing skiff from the swinging rope ladder? Being the first one down the ladder, I had to try first. The little skiff came in as close as possible and someone extended a hand. I reached for the outstretched hand and jumped, barely making it aboard, but a strong arm pulled me in through the opening. Joe was next, and then it was Marshall's turn. They made it without a problem.

As soon as we were safely aboard, Marshall asked the captain of the skiff to circle the freighter so we could see if the scratches were still there. As we approached the bow, the large scratches loomed into view, our only reminder of the crushing of our precious *Clambake*. Somehow we knew those scratches would disappear shortly. He would need to arrange for pictures to be taken while the ship traversed the locks, but he was pacified for the moment.

While Marshall was still involved talking with the captain about the evidence, I stood at the door of the skiff looking up to see if I could still see Kim and the captain. It was with tear-filled eyes that I watched the *Hanjin Savannah* vanish in the distance as our skiff sped toward the central wharf. Although we were glad to finally be on our way home, it was difficult and sad to leave the ship and the gracious men who had rescued us.

A few minutes later we arrived at the Customs dock, to be greeted by Edmund Glowen, the American ambassador in Panama. He was a round-faced, pleasant gentleman who seemed genuinely concerned about how we were doing, both physically and emotionally. After preliminary introductions, he escorted us in the back door of the Customs and Immigration office, where they took care of official paper work. He provided us with an official embossed letter from the State Department stating our names, passport numbers, and dates of birth. The letter stated that we had been in an accident at sea and all official paper work was lost. It asked for official cooperation in this matter and was signed by Glowen, the ambassador.

Embassy of the United States of America
Panama, Republic of Panama

March 26, 1993

Mr. Marshall Saunders
P.O. Box 493930
Redding, Ca. 96049

Dear Mr. Saunders:

I'm pleased to know that you finally arrived in California safe and sound. I hope your wife and Joe are recovering both physically and emotionally.

As I informed you during our telephone conversation on March 23 regarding photos of the "Hanjin Savannah", apparently the shipping agency contacted a professional photographer from the Panama Canal Commission. However, the shipping agency was not disposed to paying the $450 the photographer wanted, stating that the ship would be "surveyed" upon arrival in the U.S.

Although I talked the photographer down to $225 and finally thought he might do it free of charge, I have not heard from him subsequently. I went to the Pedro Miguel locks myself on the morning of Sunday, March 21, armed with my 35mm hand camera. Unfortunately, the "Hanjin Savannah" transited the lock most distant from the shore (there are two parallel locks). It also appears that there was some scratching of the film during developing (i.e., there are more scratches that I recall seeing with the naked eye).

The most noticeable scratch I saw on the ship was an almost horizontal line 20-30 feet long not far from the bow. In the one picture where this scratch is discernible I circled it in green ink. Perhaps you can get an enlargement of the negative, or a better quality photo.

Good luck with your claim. The shipping agent also called on March 23 and inquired as to the costs of repatriation. I informed him of the $2677.00 cost of the tickets, plus $60 airport departure tax.

Sincerely,

Edmund P. Glowen, Jr.
Consul

Enclosures:
  Photographs

At this point, he presented us with two options. "I have arranged for a hotel room for the evening, if you would like to relax before you start your journey home; or, if you prefer, I can drive you to the airport. I also made reservations for a flight that can take you back to the States today."

We chose the airline tickets and an immediate return home. Prior to our departure, Marshall asked the ambassador, "Would it be possible to arrange for someone to take pictures of the scratches on the side of the freighter as the *Hanjin* traverses the locks tomorrow morning?"

"I will make sure someone is there, and if I can't find a professional, I will be there myself to take the pictures, "he said.

He stayed with us until he was certain we had gotten through Customs with no problems. We thanked him for his help and kindness and said goodbye.

The shipping agency called a professional photographer from the Panama Canal commission to take photos of the freighter. However, the shipping agency was not disposed to paying the $450 the photographer wanted, stating that the ship would be surveyed upon arrival in the U.S. Although Glowen ultimately talked the photographer down to $225 and finally thought he might do it free of charge, he never heard from him. So, armed with his 35 mm camera, the ambassador went to the Mira Flores locks on the morning of March 21 and took the pictures himself.

Two weeks after our arrival home we received a letter with the photos of the *Hanjin Savannah* from the ambassador. We had no idea what an enormous help these would be later when we presented our case to *Hanjin*'s insurance adjuster.

Picture taken for the author by Ambassador Edmund P. Glowen Jr. of the Hanjin Savanah *freighter going through the Miraflores locks.*

A close-up picture taken for the author by Ambassador Edmund P. Glowen Jr. of damaging evidence left by Clambake's *spreaders.*

CHAPTER 14

Arrival in Florida

L OOKING RATHER MOTLEY AND CARRYING ONLY OUR WATER-
proof survival bag, we were delivered by the ambassador
to the Panama City Airport's security check station. I was still
garbed in my navy blue sweats with the Hanjin insignia em-
blazoned on the pocket and Joe was dressed in the drab green
work clothes given to him by the Korean crew. Fortunately,
Marshall now was wearing the brand new pair of jeans and shirt
provided by Kim prior to leaving the freighter. We still wore
our ill-fitting sandals.

Although our hosts aboard the freighter had been kind to
us, they did not supply us with razors, deodorant, or other personal toiletries during our five-day stay aboard their ship. Also,
they insisted that Joe and I not wash our hair because of our
head wounds. Faithfully each day, they had applied Liquid Stitch
to our gashes, so we had little plastic horns sticking out of the
side of our greasy hair. Both boys had acquired a good stubble
of beard—at least enough to look "rough"—and I was growing
some pretty good bristles on my legs. All in all, we were not the
ideal image of clean-cut American travelers.

Our hearts were beating wildly with anticipation as we approached the x-ray machine with the vision that we might wind up in a Panamanian jail. What could be more suspicious looking on the screen than a flare gun, a VHF radio, an EPIRB shaped like a bomb, and a foil rectangular package—our freeze-dried peas. Unbelievably, we passed through security without even a blink from the guard checking the screen.

The next security stop was an officious looking woman doing a frisk-down and search of carry-on bags. As far as we could tell, she had opened everyone's bag ahead of us. I was first in our group; Joe followed. We carried nothing. Marshall brought up the rear with our sole possession, the survival bag. He threw it on the counter and raised his arms above his head. She frisked him and waved him through, never opening the bag. We still don't understand why, but it made us worry a little about security checks.

We arrived in Florida that evening to find out our flight to San Francisco was overbooked by 28 people. When the airline offered a $500 voucher, plus motel and dinner expenses for each person willing to give up a seat and catch a flight the following day, we decided to accept. They shuttled us to a beach motel that was being refurbished and was undergoing a lot of construction.

With our hotel room reserved and our vouchers in hand, our first agenda was to purchase toiletries and to clean up. The hotel's gift shop was closed and the concierge directed us to a corner drug store a block away. We arrived there at 10 before 10 p.m. and the store door already was locked, with bars across it. The sign indicated the store should be open until 10, so we knocked on the door and pointed to our watches. A young man, after looking us over, let Joe and me inside; but when Marshall tried to enter, the man said no. Marshall remained outside with our survival bag.

We purchased the essentials and returned outside to find Marshall wide-eyed and aghast.

"You won't f…ing believe what just happened! While you were inside the store, I got mugged! I was leaning up against the wall checking out the surrounding buildings with all the iron bars on their windows, thinking that this must not be the best section of town when these two hoodlums approached me from out of nowhere and asked for my money. I couldn't believe it. I just stood there for a second and then I went crazy. I started yelling, "I just got run over by a 700-foot freighter, sunk in the middle of the night in the Pacific Ocean, and now you want my money. You're f…ing crazy!"

Joe and I stood there with mouths agape.

"I was past the point of being intimidated," Marshall continued. "I started swinging our survival bag over my head like I was going to let them have it. I must have looked like a madman."

"What did they do? Did they have a knife or any weapon?" I gasped.

"I didn't see any. I was yelling obscenities and telling them they picked the wrong f--ing target tonight. I just kept yelling, 'I've got no money; do I look like I've got money? I just lost everything. Get out of here!' The entire time I was swinging the bag over my head as if any second I was going to release it and let them have it."

"Where did they go?" I asked.

Marshall chuckled, "They took off running down the street; I guess I intimidated them."

Joe and I stood there, not moving, listening to Marshall's amazing story.

Finally Joe started laughing, "They must have been really hard up. Look at the three of us."

"Yeah, we are a motley looking trio, aren't we?" I agreed.

We walked toward the hotel discussing what had happened to Marshall. The more we talked about it, the more we laughed. I was eager to get back. The streets were deserted and the air was hot and humid. I was looking forward to a long, hot shower and a good night's sleep without any more adventures.

We slept soundly in the clean, warm rooms of the hotel. There was a sense of peace being back in the U.S.A. and knowing that tomorrow we would fly home to San Francisco.

The sun filtered through the curtains of the room, nudging me awake. A shiver of excitement surged through my body, knowing we were going home. Our shuttle to the airport wasn't supposed to arrive until 11 a.m. so there was plenty of time to relax. We were to meet Joe for breakfast, but earlier he had knocked on our door and told us he was going for a walk down the beach.

"I want to take a dip in the Atlantic, since we all were dipped in the Pacific Ocean last week," Joe joked.

Although Marshall and I didn't quite characterize that as a dip, we encouraged him to go for his walk. Joe took off for the beach and Marshall and I relaxed, discussing our plan of so-called "attack" upon our return home. The time flew by and when Marshall checked his watch, it was five minutes before 11 a.m.

Glancing out the window, Marshall asked, "I wonder what on earth happened to Joe?"

"Maybe he's waiting in the hotel lobby; let's go down and check," I suggested.

We searched the lobby but there was no sign of Joe. The shuttle was to arrive any minute.

"Marshall, what are we going to do if the shuttle arrives and Joe still isn't here?"

Marshall, with noticeable disgust in his voice, answered, "I don't know. I can't believe he isn't back yet."

At that moment the shuttle pulled up in front of the hotel lobby.

With hands on my hips, I turned to Marshall and asked, "What do we do now?"

Just as we were about to explain our dilemma to the shuttle driver, we saw a shirtless Joe running up the street toward the hotel. As he came into the lobby panting his explanation, the concierge approached him and said he was not allowed in the lobby without a shirt.

The concierge guided him into a back room, with us following close behind.

"They stole my shirt," Joe yelled over his shoulder in frustration.

"What does that have to do with being late?" Marshall asked, still obviously irritated.

Panting, Joe answered, "When I left the hotel on my way to the beach, I tied my shirt to the wrought iron fence so I could identify which gate I came out. I guess while I was jogging down the beach, somebody stole my shirt. The gates all look the same from the beach, so I ran right past our hotel. Half a mile down the beach, I finally figured out that I had gone too far. I can't believe somebody stole my shirt."

The concierge found a large towel and handed it to Joe. "This is what I get to wear to the airport?" Joe asked.

"Joe, come on—the van is waiting. Just wrap the towel around you. We don't want to miss the plane," Marshall said impatiently.

We arrived at the airport with Joe wrapped in a towel.

I was praying, *Please, God, no more challenges.*

With $22 left to our name—the change left over from the purchase of our airline tickets and toiletries—we bought Joe a T-shirt at one of the gift shops before boarding the plane.

Just six days after leaving Puerto Vallarta, we were on our way back home. I tried to digest the events that had transpired. The extent of our loss was becoming more obvious. I felt numb, strangely hollow. As I sorted through my feelings, the emptiness was there because, yes, we had lost everything—our home, photos of our family, my wedding rings—but they were only things. With each passing day, it was becoming more apparent to me that *things* were not what mattered in life, for they were *only things* and could be replaced.

We had lost a lot, yet I felt I had gained a new appreciation for the people in my life—for life itself. I learned that life is our most valued possession. Somehow, I knew I had changed for the better through this whole experience.

CHAPTER 15

Home At Last

THE FOUR-HOUR PLANE RIDE FROM MIAMI TO SAN FRANCISCO gave me plenty of time to reminisce about each of our daughters. I had been picturing them in my mind and savoring their accomplishments, when before I realized it, the plane landed in San Francisco. As we walked down the boarding ramp, my heart leaped. Standing at the gate was our family. Our three beautiful daughters and two sons-in-law. What a wonderful sight!

Lisa, our middle daughter, was the first to spot us. I could hear her shout, "There they are."

Our youngest flashed the largest smile I have ever seen in my life.

I could see Sheri, our eldest, standing there in her jeans and red T-shirt, anxiously scanning every passenger entering the lobby.

The moment they saw us they waved and came running to greet us. They seemed to be talking all at once.

"Welcome home. Oh, Mom, and Marshall, it's so great to see you. We're so glad you are home safe. You scared us to death."

I could see Sheri's eyes roaming over our bodies searching for obvious injuries. "See, we're all in one piece," I chided. Then I reached out for her. "You have no idea how wonderful it is to see you. I have to admit there was a moment or two that I wasn't sure I would ever see you again." I grabbed her and we hugged, with tears running down our cheeks. Soon we were *all* hugging, laughing, crying, and talking at the same time.

Joe's wife, Peggy, ran to greet him. Joe didn't say much; he just hugged her for a long time.

Lisa admitted, "We were expecting the worst when you walked off the plane; we all were sure you weren't telling the whole truth over the radio."

Nicole chimed in, "We just knew your injuries had to be worse than what you said they were and you didn't want us to worry."

Marshall put his arms around Lisa and Nicole, giving them a big squeeze. "You girls know nothing ever happens to me and your Mom. I have a Colgate shield around me."

With tears running down her face, Lisa said, "*You* have no idea what a relief it is just to see that you really are okay."

As I looked at each of them, it was almost as if I were seeing them for the first time. It was really hitting home how fortunate we had been to be given this second chance at life.

We had set their lives in turmoil since they learned of our accident via the ham radio a week earlier. On the five-hour ride home to Redding, we found out about all the calls they had made to the Coast Guard, the State Department, their local congressman, and on and on. Not only had our family been working on our behalf, but also friends from all over the States had called the girls and offered to send money, clothes, or anything else that they could do to help get us home. We were overwhelmed by their generosity; it made us realize how lucky we were to have friends who would invest hours on our behalf.

On the ride home we discussed what we had planned for the next week.

Sheri immediately offered, "Now there's no arguing, you are staying at our house until you get things in order."

"That would be wonderful, honey, but do you mind if we set up our camper in your driveway? That way we both can have a little privacy."

"Of course not, but when your 11-foot camper gets small, you are welcome to stay in the house."

With that settled, we continued to answer a gazillion questions about the accident and our time aboard the freighter. The long ride home went by quickly, and when we passed the sign saying five miles to Redding, I realized how exhausted I was. I was going to sleep really well that night, having all of my family around me. It felt great to be home.

Marshall got up early the next day. He was eager to see most of our problems behind us, so he immediately began dealing with the phone calls. We set up our office in Sheri's living room when she and her husband, Jon, went off to work. We set up a team, with Marshall doing the phone calling and verbal communication while I took on the diary and daily written communication. We were used to working this way from our business, so it took on a natural flow as the weeks progressed.

We had lost everything—our home and all of our possessions. Everything that *used* to be important to us, from family photos to Marshall's favorite recipes, was lying in 3,000 feet of water somewhere in the Pacific Ocean. It was time for major decisions, time to start rebuilding both our home and our confidence to continue our lifestyle and our dream . . . or else make a decision to return to life on land.

Marshall's first call was to Florida, to our insurance company. He dialed the Lawrence Co. number and was transferred to Debbie Morales, our newly assigned claims adjuster. She guided Marshall through the process.

"First, I will need the accident report from the Coast Guard," she instructed Marshall.

"Okay, do I mail that to you?" Marshall asked.

"No, you will mail that to our adjuster in Washington, along with an itemized list of everything you lost and its value."

Marshall was given the name and phone number of the adjuster. Besides sending him the paper work, Marshall was to contact the adjuster and set up a time for a phone deposition.

Marshall then questioned Debbie as to the possibility of pursuing the Hanjin Company for the remainder of our loss. The amount not covered by insurance was substantial. When we left on our trip we had taken out insurance only on our hull, in the approximate amount of $160,000. Full coverage is very expensive for sailors traveling offshore into foreign countries. Never in our wildest dreams did we expect to have a total loss of our boat.

Debbie officiously responded, "No, you can't pursue the Hanjin Co. because of the subrogation rights, the rights of priority of recovery from others, that is covered in your policy. That would definitely create a conflict of interest."

Before finishing the conversation, Debbie instructed Marshall to make appointments for each of us to be examined by our family physician. Debbie would need a full report on the physical condition of all three of us. Marshall agreed to call her in a couple of days to keep her apprised of our progress in getting reports to the Washington adjuster.

"That was very discouraging information," he said glumly. "She said we can't pursue the Hanjin Company because of subrogation rights. We'll have to research that some more. That doesn't seem right."

I was aghast. The amount not covered by insurance was substantial. We probably had close to $375,000 into our boat and possessions. During those last few years prior to our retirement, we had lavished *Clambake* with everything imaginable. We had five cameras—a good 35 mm, a Polaroid, a VCR, an underwater Instamatic, and an inexpensive Instamatic—two folding Montague bikes . . . and so it was with a hundred other items and gadgets. *How will we ever be able to replace* Clambake *and all her equipment with only $160,000?* I wondered.

"I agree, we'll have to research what these subrogation rights are and why we can't talk to Hanjin about our loss. That could be disastrous for us. Things are not off to a good start, are they?" I asked. "Thank heavens we still have our rentals to provide us with monthly income."

Suddenly a thought occurred to me. "Marshall, what would you think of driving to San Francisco to pick up the report in person? You know how government agencies can be; the request could sit on somebody's desk for weeks before it gets mailed."

"I think it's a great idea," he agreed. We had learned in the real estate business that it always paid off when we did things in person, as opposed to by phone or mail. We also learned that it was especially important to negotiate in person. It's a lot harder for a person to say no when they are looking across the table from you than over the phone.

Even though Debbie Morales advised us of a conflict in interest, we decided Marshall's second call that day would be to the Hanjin Shipping Co. The captain had followed through with his promise before we left the ship and provided the name and phone number of a man at its New York office. Marshall dialed the number and after a few transfers, got through to a Mr. Bae. He told Marshall, "Nobody has given me any information on your case. I will have to make some calls. Would you please call back tomorrow?"

Marshall hung up the phone looking very discouraged. "I think I'm getting the run-around. This one isn't going to be easy. Are you in the middle of something? I'd like to talk for a minute."

"Sure, what's on your mind?"

"Ya' know, Dee, we will be bitter and old if we have to take this to court and have to relive this accident daily for the next three years. We need to make an effort to talk to someone in the Hanjin Co. We need to find someone who will sit down and talk with us, and we need to be ready to make compromises and get on with our dream while we still are in good health and able to do the cruising."

"I agree with you 100 percent. There is no reason to go to court. I don't want to be made rich from this accident, and I know you don't, either. I just want to be back to the position we were on March 15th, with a boat that is seaworthy so we can continue with our dream, and do it as soon as possible. The question is, how do we find that person in the company, and second, if we find him, how do we get him to sit down with us and discuss our accident?"

We had many hours on the freighter to talk about how we were going to handle things once we arrived home. What we didn't anticipate was how difficult it would be to find someone with whom we could discuss our losses. We honestly felt we could accomplish more in person by talking with the right people, and in a much shorter time than an attorney could going through the legal system. Negotiating was what we had done for our livelihood for the last 13 years. We were good at it; we worked well as a team.

Even with the minimal court involvement we had in our real estate business, we found that the stress in going to court was high; it was something we preferred to avoid if at all possible. We found that even insignificant cases could drag on for more than a year. It always seemed that the process consumed lots of wasteful, negative energy. We wanted to proceed with a positive attitude.

We knew we would need to hire an attorney to guide us and review all paperwork. We certainly didn't know anything about maritime law, and insurance policies always were a nightmare to decipher. We already were getting a taste of our ineptness with the "subrogation rights" that Debbie Morales talked about. Our hope was that a good maritime attorney would keep us from signing anything that would be a fatal mistake.

Our next phone call was a ham radio patch to one of our cruising friends on the 0900 net.

"I don't know if you heard, but there are rumors flying around on the net that Lawrence Co. might be going belly-up," Greg, our cruising friend told us.

"No, we haven't heard. What's going on?" Marshall asked. "I know the majority of the cruisers are insured with them—that could be devastating."

Greg continued, "I guess there have been a ton of claims from Hurricane Hugo. You know it struck the East Coast a few weeks ago, and I guess the claims are astronomical. I've also heard complaints that the company is really slow in settling them."

Marshall moaned, "Well, that definitely gives us something else to worry about. Will our insurance company go belly-up before we are able to collect the full $160,000?"

Marshall hung up the phone, discouraged. "Isn't *that* great news? If Lawrence really is having problems, that could mean delays for us in getting our settlement and re-establishing our lives—or even worse, it could mean we might not get any settlement at all! Dee, your idea to drive to San Francisco to do things in person really makes sense now. We need to get all this paper work in as soon as possible. Armed with the information from Greg, we need to do whatever we can in person to expedite the process."

The apprehensions we were beginning to feel after only a couple of phone calls on our first day home, were almost worse than the accident itself. We had no control over the decisions of the two large companies we had to deal with, though the outcome of each certainly would determine our future. What *if* our insurance company became insolvent and couldn't pay us? What *if* we were unable to talk to anyone at Hanjin?

So many questions were going through our minds, but one thing we both knew was that we had to continue with a positive attitude and forge ahead, solving one problem at a time.

Our next job was to find a good maritime attorney. Luckily, our youngest daughter, Nicole, had a good friend whose father was a maritime attorney. We called Nicole and asked for her help.

"I'll get the number and call you right back. It makes me feel so good I can do something to help."

A short while later with the number in hand, Marshall called Jay's father. Although he was unable to handle our case, he recommended someone in San Francisco who could. One more call and we had an appointment to meet with Gary Sterling of Number One Bush Street, San Francisco, Friday morning.

After setting up the appointments Debbie Morales had requested with our family doctor and the chiropractor, we were through with what we could do by phone the first day. Oddly enough, a couple of days later we got a call from a woman named Marie. She was an adjuster for Britannia, hired by Hanjin, and she also requested that we set up a doctor's appointment to be thoroughly checked. We told her we were scheduled to see our family doctor the following day. She said she would be in touch.

The first week home we spent a lot of time with friends and family, appreciating the gift of life and love shared. It was good therapy for us to tell the story, and of course, everyone wanted to hear every last detail.

We also spent countless hours with our friend, Joe. Although he never mentioned it, Peggy, his wife, told us he was going through a lot of emotions and guilt over the accident. He was spending some time in counseling, and it was critical for him and for us to spend as much time together talking as possible. We would reminisce and joke about the humorous things that happened, like my experience with the Korean cook or Marshall's encounter with the hoodlums in Miami. We tried to keep a positive attitude when around Joe. Marshall always made a special effort to be up in spirits, and reiterate time after time that responsibility of the accident was his: He was the captain. But we knew it was going to be a long healing process for Joe. He felt responsible for the accident. In his mind, there was no possible way to fix what had been done.

Joe always had been accident-prone. In fact, his family joked that a life-insurance policy on Joe would be a better bet than a state lottery ticket. However, in the past, he always had been able to buy a new bike for the one he drove over the ditch, or a new outboard engine for the one he buried in the sand. It was difficult for Joe to accept that this time he could not fix the problem financially.

It seemed Joe found an excuse to stop by every day. "How's it goin', guys?" he would yell as he came through the door. "Anything new to report?"

Marshall would answer back, "Hey, ol' buddy, come on in. Things are going good. Sit down, and we'll tell you about it. How are your ribs doing today, any better?"

And so the conversation went each day. He needed to know we were getting through this and doing okay, also. I think it helped when we filled him in on details of the day—

the progress, the setbacks, and the plans we had for tomorrow. It was obvious he was searching for a way to release his guilt.

My heart went out to him, but there was nothing we could say that hadn't already been said. He would sit there, quietly listening, but never added much to the conversation. His whole demeanor cried out for help. He was not the upbeat, gregarious Joe we used to know.

It also was difficult for Marshall, but in a different way. First, there was the period of disbelief, then grief, and finally anger at the loss. For Marshall, losing the boat was similar to losing a loved one. All the emotions of death were felt and had to be dealt with. Even though he was dealing with these personal issues and emotions, Marshall always tried to conceal his true feelings around Joe. He put on a positive front.

However, around me Marshall emptied his soul. I was happy to be the vessel into which he poured his fears and frustrations. It gave me a sense of fulfillment in knowing that he needed my strengths now as much as I had needed his the night of the accident.

It was obvious to me that Marshall was feeling a lot of anger, both at himself for his mistakes, and toward Joe. I felt that I needed to warn Joe.

One day I had the opportunity to talk to Joe alone and told him, "Joe, you know Marshall and I are positive people. We are going to get through this, and we *will* continue with our cruising. However, I want you to be prepared. At some point Marshall is going to have to get some anger out. When he does, I want you to know that we both still love and respect you as a friend, and what has happened will *never* affect our friendship. I just want you to be prepared when that day comes." I gave Joe a big hug as I saw tears well up in his eyes.

Joe simply nodded in acknowledgement.

When Joe wasn't around, Marshall would question how in God's name it was that Joe didn't see the freighter. Marshall was sure Joe had dozed off.

"What bothers me . . ." Marshall paused in thought and then, visibly frustrated, continued, " . . . is if Joe saw the freighter's lights behind us, obviously those lights had to have been in *front* of us at some point, if they were going in the opposite direction. Why didn't he think about where the boat was coming from or had been?"

"Ask Joe," I suggested again.

Marshall finally got the courage to ask Joe the question that was going through all of our minds. "Do you think you might have fallen asleep?"

Joe answered, "No, I was reading a book Peggy had packed for me. I saw lights way off in the distance, off our starboard transom about 10 minutes before the accident, but I thought the ship was going the other way. The next thing I remember was just feeling a presence. I looked up and saw the freighter right on our transom. I tried turning the wheel. I don't remember anything else."

Marshall would never ask Joe the question again. He was too good a friend, and at this point it didn't matter. What happened could not be changed.

Marshall had always respected Joe as an extremely capable and excellent racing skipper who seemed to have an intuitive sense for wind shifts and reading the water. He believed Joe was as least as good as, if not better, in racing, than he was and definitely looked at him as an equal as far as his skipper capabilities were concerned. That was a huge compliment, coming from Marshall. Before I met him, Marshall had done extensive racing in Hawaii on 50-foot sailboats, and was very well known in the Hawaii yacht club circle for his excellent and aggressive racing capabilities. He was considered a formidable challenger.

What really was gnawing at Marshall was the fact that he had made a big mistake in assuming Joe's abilities as a skipper included navigation and open ocean skills. He was angry with himself for not having been more intuitive and for not going over basics with Joe before we left Puerto Vallarta. Even though Joe was an excellent sailor, he had had little experience on the open ocean or in navigation.

Marshall didn't want to insult Joe's intelligence and so didn't spend the time before we left Puerto Vallarta to instruct Joe on what was important to look for on a watch, or if you saw a freighter, how to analyze what direction the other ship was going and if you were on a collision course. He now realized his lack of instructions beforehand made him as much at fault as Joe. Although he hated to admit it, he was very angry with himself for being so lax and making such a fatal mistake.

Marshall also feared there was a real possibility that we would not be able to replace *Clambake* with as nice a boat as our Tayana. *Clambake* represented all our years of hard work and our financial success in our career. With her gone, Marshall believed that so was his successful image. He was very proud of her. Hardly a day went by that someone didn't compliment us on what a beautiful boat she was and how meticulously she was maintained. She was sleek and sexy, with a gorgeous, long sheerline. It would be really difficult to find another boat that could ever come close to replacing *Clambake* in Marshall's eyes. Even more difficult would be having to take a step down in size, or backward financially.

However, to continue with our dream there was the real possibility that we *would* have to settle for a much smaller or less-expensive boat. After all, we had been taught twice that it's not the material things in life that matter—first when we lost Tiffany, and now with our accident. The priority had to be getting back out there and doing what we had worked so hard to accomplish. It was not how prestigious the boat or how lavishly we furnished her; it was getting out there and living our dream that mattered.

I can remember Marshall telling me many a time as we sat in a harbor looking enviously at the big boats across the way, "Ya' know, Dee, when I look across at that million-dollar boat over there and the people sitting on their back deck, it's hard to imagine that they can be having any more fun or enjoying it more than we are."

Even though it was generally Marshall reminding me how fortunate we were to have what we had and to be doing what we were doing at our age, occasionally I had to remind him of what he once said. I knew if we kept plugging away, one problem at a time, it wouldn't be long before we would back on another boat doing what we both loved so much—*getting out there cruising*. I knew it as sure as I knew *Clambake* was at the bottom of the ocean.

Although for the most part, Marshall, Joe, and I skirted talking about our emotions, we spent hours going over the accident trying to figure it out, replaying exactly what happened. There were still some details that didn't make sense. We pondered these issues, trying to solve the mysteries.

As it turned out, our tragedy in the ocean turned out to be good fortune for us. Several of the boats that left shortly after us to make the crossing that year got caught in a terrible storm off the coast of New Zealand. Ten boats were lost and the New Zealand Coast Guard made many heroic rescues. They responded to 19 Maydays, putting their own lives in serious jeopardy. One family was not that lucky; not only was their boat lost, but also the husband and two children were lost at sea. The wife was found alone, washed up in an inflatable raft on an island in New Zealand with many injuries and horrible memories of that ill-fated day. I'm not sure I would have had the strength to carry on as she did if any one of us had not survived our accident.

CHAPTER 16

Fearing the Outcome

MARSHALL AGAIN WAS UP EARLY BECAUSE HE HAD ARRANGED for the adjuster in Washington to call him at 9 o'clock to take the deposition that Debbie Morales had requested. That simply involved detailed questions about the accident, our boat, and some general questions about our personal possessions.

As soon as the deposition was over, Marshall tried calling Mr. Bae of Hanjin in New York. This time Mr. Bae gave Marshall the name and phone number of Mr. Soon, a man in Long Beach who reportedly had started a file on us. Marshall tried to call Mr. Soon immediately, but he was out of the office, and the secretary asked Marshall to call back later in the day. Marshall finally reached him late in the afternoon.

"Marshall Saunders: The name doesn't ring a bell. What did you say, that you were involved with some sort of accident with one of our ships? No one has given me any information on this. This is the first I have heard about any accident. Who asked you to call me, again?"

"A Mr. Bae from your New York office told me you had a file started on us, and that you would be able to arrange a meeting with my wife and me," Marshall patiently responded.

"No, I've never heard of you, and I have no file, and right at the moment I'm running late for a meeting, so I'll have to get back to you later. What is your name, again? I'll turn you over to my secretary and she can get your phone number. Hang on."

Marshall gave the secretary our number, then pushed down the button on the receiver and laid the phone in his lap, as if deciding what his next move should be. He looked at me and said in exasperation, "I'm getting the run-around again. Right about now, I'd like to get some C-4 explosives, blow a hole in their hull, and watch them sink to the bottom. Then maybe I could get somebody to talk to me."

"These calls are scaring me, Marshall. It's so hard not knowing what direction fate is going to carry us. I feel that we are so helpless and at the total mercy of these large corporations."

"I know what you mean. I don't like this feeling of not being in control."

Terrible pangs of fear were enveloping us. We started to worry where our lives would end up. First there was the rumor from Greg that our insurance company might be going under, and so far we had been unsuccessful in finding anyone to talk to at Hanjin. A million questions were running through our minds. Where and what would be home? What if we couldn't get anyone to talk to us and therefore couldn't resolve the issues between Hanjin and ourselves? How much money would we ultimately have to work with, and what could we afford in the way of a boat? Had our dream of early retirement and cruising the world just been washed out to sea? We were going to have to come up with a new approach?

The next day we saw our doctors, the following day we were scheduled to meet with the Coast Guard in San Francisco, and Friday we had our first meeting with our attorney. Maybe on the five-hour drive to San Francisco, we could come up with a new plan on how to handle Hanjin.

The doctor's appointment was uneventful; he said my head wound was healing fine but ordered an MRI to check for fractures. There still were some rope burns on my legs from the lines that had wrapped around my calf as *Clambake* was sinking, but they also were healing and showed no sign of infection. He confirmed that Marshall probably had broken his nose, but there didn't appear to be any obstruction, so there was nothing he could do for it. The MRI on my skull showed nothing unusual.

Thursday morning we drove to the Coast Guard station in Alameda and pulled up to the gate to check in as instructed. A guard in a starched gray uniform stepped forward. Marshall rolled down his window and explained that we were here to file an accident report.

"One moment, sir. I need to call my commanding officer for further instructions."

The officer stepped back into the guardhouse. After hanging up the phone he bent forward and asked, "May I please see your driver's license or some other form of picture identification?"

Marshall leaned out of the window and handed him our gold-embossed letter from the Ambassador. "We were in an accident at sea and lost all identification. This letter from the Panamanian Ambassador explains it."

The guard took the letter, scrutinized it, and responded, "I'll have to call my commanding officer back. This doesn't have any picture ID. I can't let you on the base with only this as identification."

We waited while he again talked to his commanding officer. Shortly, he leaned back over toward the car and peered through the window, obviously checking us over.

"Sir, my commanding officer has instructed me to inform you that since you can't produce a driver's license with picture identity, you will have to park your car outside the base and walk in."

This was not getting off to a good start, but we parked the car outside the gate and walked the half-mile to a large drab office building. We found our way to the Marine Safety Office and were directed to a small cubicle where the officer in charge was going to be doing the interviewing. We didn't know what to expect, but were prepared to be reprimanded for the accident. We were pleasantly surprised to find a tall, friendly looking man enter the cubicle. He introduced himself and sat down behind the old metal desk across from us. The officer, a sympathetic man, was interested in every detail of the accident that we could remember.

After several hours of conversation and filling out reports, the officer placed the pen down on his desk and leaned forward. "I don't know if you were aware of this, but on the night of your accident, the Coast Guard had a C-120 sitting on the runway in Sacramento with a full crew ready to be deployed. We were having trouble getting permission to refuel in Mexico because the Mexican government felt it was the primary rescue agent." He leaned back in his chair and with a slight, almost sarcastic smile, continued on, "As it turned out, the *Hanjin Savannah* had rescued you and notified the Coast Guard before the government red tape was resolved."

Marshall and I exchanged glances. "We had no idea the Coast Guard was even aware of our accident. It's reassuring to know that they were ready to act if needed," responded Marshall.

The officer took a minute to look over his notes and said, "You mentioned you had activated an EPIRB that night, correct?"

"That's correct," Marshall responded.

"We never received your signal."

"We had an inkling of that when our daughter told us she was never notified. She is the primary name listed to contact in an emergency."

"Do you recall when you activated the EPIRB that evening?"

"Yes, I know exactly when we activated it. It was while we were still on *Clambake*, before she went down; we had it on the entire time we were on the life raft, and didn't remember to turn it off until we were up in Hanjin's infirmary."

"About how long would you say that was?"

"That had to be close to an hour and a half," Marshall answered. "It was blinking the entire time, so we assumed it was working."

"I assume the unit was left on the *Hanjin Savannah*?" the officer asked.

"As a matter of fact, we still have the unit," Marshall responded.

Surprised, the officer asked, "Would you mind sending the EPIRB to us? We're very curious why it didn't work, so I would like to run some tests to find out why your signal was never received."

"So would we. That's a real mystery. There were six of us cruisers who purchased them prior to leaving Puerto Vallarta. If they were defective, it would be nice to know so we could warn the others. As soon as we get back to Redding, we'll send it to you."

The officer apologized for the inconvenience of our having to walk in to his office. He wished us well with our insurance claim and negotiations with Hanjin, and asked us to stop at the documentation office on the way out to file a form stating, "There no longer is a vessel named *Clambake*."

We entered the stark office one floor below and got into line and waited. When it was our turn, we explained to the clerk that we had been sent there to sign an official statement declaring that *Clambake* was lost at sea.

It was really hitting home now. *Clambake* was gone forever. She soon would be officially buried in the archives of Coast

Guard documentation. Little did we realize that when we initially signed what seemed like a pound of papers to purchase *Clambake,* promising till "death do us part." Eight years later we would be signing one little document stating *Clambak*e no longer existed. We could not have guessed that the parting would be this painful, or so final.

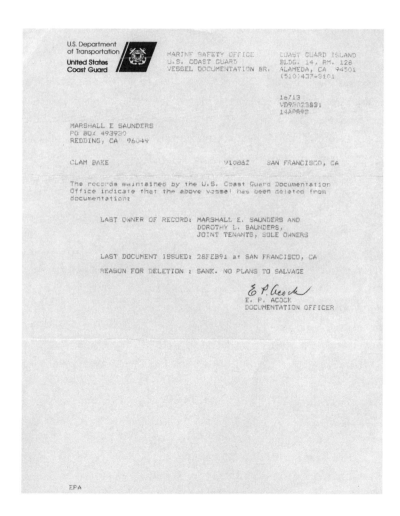

The following day we met our new attorney. Our trip to his office was overwhelming. We knew we were in big trouble as we stepped out of the elevator on the seventh floor and looked out over San Francisco through the large plate-glass windows.

Marshall leaned over to me and whispered, "We're in the wrong place; we're way out of our league. There is no way we can afford this guy."

"Yeah, you're right, but we're here and he's expecting us, so I guess we should go through with today's appointment."

We initially met with two partners from the firm, but eventually were turned over to Gary Sterling, the senior of the two. As we followed him into his private office, I observed that he was dressed immaculately in a pin-stripe suit that reeked the word "expensive." He was of medium height and build and had salt-and-pepper hair, but his slightly protruding stomach and rosy cheeks diminished any distinguishing features he might have had. Yet he looked and acted the part of a very successful attorney. He could have been cast into any movie scene as such a character.

We told our story, with several interruptions from Gary asking specific questions. When we finished, he leaned back in his chair and with a deep, slow drawl said, "Maritime law is very different from civil law. There is never 100 percent right or wrong. Each party has a percentage of fault, otherwise there never would have been an accident. However, I think you have a strong case, and I would be interested in taking it on a contingency basis."

Marshall and I glanced at each other in surprise. Then Marshall cautiously asked, "Why would you want to take our case on a contingency basis?"

"I've been an attorney for some 20-plus years. Most of my cases involve big companies—for example, *Sony vs. Hanjin*— usually over some containers that were damaged or lost at sea. I just finished a case where an aircraft carrier and passenger liner collided. It's one big company against another.

"Your case doesn't involve a container full of things. This is something that is real. You are real people with a real problem, and it would be very gratifying emotionally for me to help you—and a nice change of pace."

"We appreciate your generous offer to take our case on contingency; however, Dee and I have discussed going to court over this, and we decided we don't want to do that. We feel that if we can find the right person to talk to in the Hanjin Co., we can resolve the issues a lot faster sitting down at a round table and discussing it. We simply would like to hire an attorney to prevent us from making any fatal errors."

Gary leaned back in his chair and carefully responded, "I've dealt with the Hanjin Company before. They are not easy to deal with and their adjusters are very slow to resolve issues. You will need someone to represent you who not only is knowledgeable in maritime law, but also in international law."

We listened intently to what Gary was saying. Then Marshall couldn't resist asking, "If I were your favorite grandmother, what would you advise *her* to do?"

With palms pressed together and fingers interlocked, Gary looked down at his desk and thought for a moment. "Well, I will tell you what I will do for you, and this would be what I would also advise my favorite grandmother to do," he chuckled.

"We can work together on an hourly rate for the first 90 days, with the two of you doing all the negotiating. I will review all paperwork to be signed, whether it is from the insurance company or the Hanjin Shipping Co. I feel quite certain that you will not be able to accomplish much with Hanjin in 90 days. After that time I will switch to taking on your case on a contingency basis. How does that sound to you?"

Marshall and I glanced at each other again, and Marshall understood by my look that I agreed with that proposal. Marshall then asked Gary what his hourly rate would be.

After we came to that agreement, Gary told us he would draw up a contract and send it to our Redding address. Meanwhile, he was going to talk to the Lawrence Co., and try and get us copies of the Coast Guard reports.

In days to come, it turned out that Gary was invaluable to us in catching critical mistakes in the paperwork. One mistake originated with Lawrence Insurance Co. It would have prevented us from pursuing our claim against Hanjin. Later, Gary found another critical mistake against Hanjin in regard to the subrogation rights of our insurance company.

We left his office with mixed emotions that first day and decided to go have a bite to eat and discuss what had transpired during the last hour. We found a little café down the street and stepped inside to a small, quiet booth where we could privately discuss our meeting with Gary.

"Well, what did you think about all of that?" Marshall asked once we got seated.

"I was really amazed that he offered to take the case on a contingency basis, weren't you?"

"Yeah, that did throw me a curve. At first I couldn't figure out why he would make that offer, but after talking with him for a while, I had the feeling he genuinely liked us and wants to help us. I also think that possibly he believes that there might be some money to be made in this case. He never said that today, but I can't believe his motivation is all purely benevolent."

"I agree. I sure like the idea of having 90 days to work on things on our own. Weren't you happy with that offer?"

"Yes, I thought that was very fair on his part, although I was a little discouraged that he felt we couldn't solve our problems in 90 days."

"Me, too. He sure wasn't very encouraging in that regard, but I think he is very knowledgeable. He certainly has lots of years of experience in maritime law. I think we are fortunate to have his referral from Jay's dad. At least, I feel comfortable that he will keep us from making any fatal errors."

"More important, he seemed confident that with 'time' we could get some settlement from Hanjin. That sure made me feel better after the run-around we have been getting from them last week. The question is, how much time are we willing to give up to come out whole?"

We knew the answer to this question in our hearts. We wanted to be back on the water, living our dream. We did not want to spend years in the courtroom.

Before we went back to Redding, we decided that as long as we were in the Bay Area, we should try to look at a few boats. We stumbled into one brokerage and met Jim, an enthusiastic salesman who appeared to have good knowledge of the local inventory. He had several boats he could show us under $150,000. We decided to stay a couple of extra days, and called our friends John and Shari, to see if they would like to go boat-hunting with us over the weekend. They joined us Friday evening.

We met Jim early Saturday at the Alameda docks, where he showed us the first boat, a one-off New Zealand steel boat. Looking at it was very discouraging; it was commodious, but in terrible condition. Marshall's immediate concern was that it wasn't a performance cruiser and wouldn't sail very well to weather. We continued to look at boats all day with Jim, and by the end of the afternoon we realized we would have to up the price range to $200,000. Nothing we looked at came close to being of interest to us.

We started out Sunday morning refreshed and eager to look at more expensive boats. With each boat Jim showed us, we became more and more discouraged. Either they were in bad shape and in need of lots of work, or they were much smaller than *Clambake*.

Halfway through the second day, after looking at an older Vagabond 47, I broke down in tears. In my mind, none of the boats we had seen came close to comparing with our beloved *Clambake*. I was beginning to think we would never find another boat that could truly make us happy and that we could call home. While I was feeling frustration, Marshall was becoming impatient with looking. By the end of the day, he started to think that any boat would work, even the ones *without* a modern hull underbody or ones that were in terrible condition.

Over dinner we discussed the different boats we had seen. I was determined to point out to Shari why I was so distraught. It was that none of the boats came close to having the amenities *Clambake* had. Instead of sympathizing with me, she started pointing out positive features in the boats that we viewed. She made quite a few inferences that *Clambake* was not perfect, either. Both Shari and John believed a couple of the boats had definite potential.

At first I was angry that my good friend didn't empathize and agree with me. But after I took time to think about what she had said, I realized she was right, and that it took a really good friend to be brave enough to point this out to me. From that day on, thanks to Shari's honesty, I was able to look at boats with a different and more open point of view.

It was over this weekend, also, that I came to realize I had developed claustrophobia. Small places or dark rooms had never bothered me before the accident. However, while looking at boats, I had a desperate feeling of needing air every time I went below in a boat that had small or few escape hatches.

On one of the older, darker boats we previewed, I had to make a mad dash to get topside. I can remember calling to Marshall, "I need to get out of here quick."

"What's wrong?" he looked concerned.

"I don't know. I just need fresh air," I responded, panicking.

My hands had started to sweat, my heart was beating rapidly, and I felt I couldn't breathe. I realized at that moment that it would be essential for our next boat to have large escape hatches and a bright, airy feeling in every cabin.

Even while riding in the elevator at the hotel, a panicky suffocating feeling overtook me; I found myself walking the stairs whenever possible.

This appeared to be the only after-effect of the accident either Marshall or I suffered. We never had nightmares or fears of returning to cruising the oceans. Now our only fear was whether we could find a boat that would make us both happy; and if we could, would we have the money to pay for it?

CHAPTER 17

Rebuilding Our Identities

ONCE THE INSURANCE PROCESS WAS IN MOTION AND WE had set up all other appointments we believed were immediately necessary, we undertook the task of obtaining new drivers' licenses, passports, and so on. Our first stop was at the Department of Motor Vehicles. After we had gone through a brief version of our tale of woe and showed the clerk the letter from the State Department, she explained that without further identification, the Department of Motor Vehicles had no way of knowing we really were the Saunders, and could not reissue our drivers' licenses. We left the office a little dejected, but figured that we could *certainly* establish our identity. We would get our passports—that should work.

On the way to the county clerk's office to obtain new passports, we stopped at the post office to get a new box key. We met with the same discouraging objections there, and so left with no key to our box and obviously, no mail.

We briefly sat in the car planning our next move. Mutually we decided our next stop should be the county clerk's office. This was getting ridiculous. Surely we shouldn't have a problem there, with the official letter we had from the ambassador's office. It even identified each of us, giving our birthdates and passport numbers.

Guess what? Even after our story of woe and presentation of our State Department letter, we were firmly told that the only way we could obtain a new passport was to produce birth certificates or bring back two friends or relatives who were willing to sign affidavits that we were who we claimed to be.

I turned to Marshall, and I could feel the tears welling up in my eyes. "That isn't going to work. The kids can't come to sign affidavits—they all have jobs during normal business hours— and our birth certificates will take weeks to get by mail."

"Now wipe away those tears; we'll figure out something," he tried to comfort me.

Marshall's sympathetic actions merely stimulated a water fall of tears. I couldn't stop sobbing.

Embarrassed, I turned away. This wasn't like me. Normally, I'm a strong person. But this insignificant incident with the county clerk had been just enough frustration to let all of my pent-up emotions from the last two weeks' events let loose. It was as if somebody had pulled a plug out of a dike. I couldn't help myself.

After Marshall took me aside and tried to calm me, he again tried to explain our frustration to the clerk.

"You see, we lost everything when our boat went down, and we would have to send back to Pennsylvania for new birth certificates, which will take considerable time. The Ambassador from Panama told us that this letter from the State Department with our passport numbers right here would pave the way to expedite the process."

All of this was to no avail. The clerk's feet were firmly planted when she repeated her programmed answer. At least this time there was a little empathy in her voice when she said "I'm sorry."

We left the office silently, with no ID.

Suddenly a spark came into Marshall's eye. "I have a thought," he said, flashing me a knowing smile.

Without explanation he headed to the other side of town and pulled into the Costco parking lot. Lo and behold, 10 minutes later we were standing in Costco holding new picture ID cards.

Now laughing, we flew back to the post office. Aha! No problem now getting a key to our box, with our new picture ID.

Dare we try DMV? Why not? We were on a roll.

By the end of the day we were on our way to re-establishing all of our lost ID, thanks to Costco's computer, which still had us on file.

CHAPTER 18

The Negotiations

THE NEXT FEW WEEKS BROUGHT MORE FRUSTRATION. Our emotions roller-coasted up and down, from highs to lows, depending on how our phone conversations went with the insurance company and Hanjin. The shipping company was especially frustrating. We still were getting the run-around. Our first call to Mr. Bae in New York had led us to Mr. Soon in Long Beach, who referred us to someone in Los Angeles, who in turn referred us to someone in Puson, Korea. We tried numerous times to call Korea but got cut off by the operator, and when we finally got through, the gentleman hung up on us, probably because he didn't understand English and we didn't understand or could not speak Korean.

Marshall's conversation with each of them always started out explaining our accident at sea with one of their ships. He then indicated we wanted to be able to sit down with someone in the company who had authority to discuss our loss and come to an equitable agreement for both of us. The answer had always been the same—"You will need to talk to Mr. Blankity-Blank in our Blankity-Blank office"—and we would be shuffled to one more new person.

"I'm beginning to think Gary was right. We're getting nowhere with Hanjin. If only we could find someone who would sit down with us and talk, I know we could make progress," said Marshall, obviously frustrated.

"Maybe we need a diversion for a week or so," I suggested. I had been sitting across from him at Sheri's table organizing our paperwork.

"We were planning to drive up to Seattle to meet with the adjuster in person and deliver all this." I pointed to the stacks of paper neatly organized in front of me. "Maybe we could continue up to the San Juan Islands and visit with your brother, Craig, and his wife, Linda, for a few days and look at a few boats in the Seattle area. Isn't Craig scheduled for some exploratory heart surgery this next week?"

"Yeah, I think he is."

"Well, maybe we can see if he would be up for some company and moral support when he goes in for the surgery; I think it might be good for us to get our thoughts off of our own problems for awhile. Also, I think Hanjin has an office in Seattle. I can compose a letter to the chairman of the board and we could drop by that office and get his fax number and send it. Who knows, maybe we'll get lucky and find someone there who speaks *English* and will talk to us. We aren't getting any results at the lower levels, so why not go directly to the top?" I suggested to Marshall.

"Not a bad idea. It would be good to see Craig and Linda. I'd like to be there with him when he goes in for the surgery, if he doesn't mind the company. Maybe after visiting with Craig we can also stop and talk to Robert Perry. His office is in Seattle, and since he designed *Clambake*, maybe he can give us a few suggestions of some different boats to look at that would be similar to the Tayana."

I had found the Hanjin chairman's name in a brochure lying on a coffee table in the recreation room while we were on board the freighter. I had written it my notes on one of those days after we had paraded on our walk. I never expected that we would need it, but now it seemed like a possible approach to get someone's attention.

I dug through my notes, found his name, and composed the following letter. My thought was that perhaps we could get someone in that Seattle office to fax it directly to him in Puson, Korea.

Chairman Cho Choon Hoon
Hanjin Shipping Co.
Pusan, South Korea

Dear Mr. Cho:

This letter is to inform you of the numerous attempts we have made to discuss our loss at sea with people in your company. Our first contact with your company was initiated two days after the collision. Since that time we have spoken with Mr. Bae and Mr. Soon on numerous occasions, requesting the name of someone to communicate with to discuss our loss. To date, we still do not have a name. Due to the fact that we have been unsuccessful in our attempts, we are bringing it to "your" attention in hopes that you might be willing to help us.

March 16 our yacht Clambake, under full sail, was hit in the stern and sunk by the Hanjin Savannah off the coast of Mexico at approximately 12:45 a.m. The same vessel rescued us, and for that we are very grateful. The captain and crew were most courteous to us and did what they could to help with our injuries.

We officially moved onto our 50-foot sailing vessel Clambake in January 1991, after selling our business and our home. At that time we moved everything of value onto the boat with us, for it was "home," where we worked, entertained, and played, and it symbolized all our achievements of our working life.

One month has passed and we still know nothing more than the day of the accident. We are still "homeless" and waiting for someone to talk to. We're feeling frustrated, angry, and robbed of the life we have worked so hard to achieve. We are not looking for sympathy, but hope that the Hanjin Company can see that we are real people put through the trauma of losing our home and almost our lives, and that it will treat us with more compassion than a damaged freight claim.

We look to you, Mr. Cho, and your expert advice on how we can expedite these thoughts to the people in your company to settle this matter in a manner efficient and beneficial for both of us. We are most anxious to hear from you. You can contact us directly at 9xx-xxx-xxxx.

Sincerely,
Marshall and Dee Saunders

April 14th, almost one month after our accident, we walked into the Seattle Hanjin office and asked the receptionist at the main desk if she could provide us with the chairman's fax number.

The receptionist was curious why two people walking in off the street would want the chairman's fax number. We poured forth our tale of the accident.

She was flabbergasted with our story, and within minutes had on the phone a gentleman from Long Beach whom she said would be able to help us.

Dubious, Marshall took the phone. "Hello, this is Marshall Saunders speaking."

"Hello, Marshall. My name is Mr. Barzin. I'm head of the claims department for Hanjin. I understand you had an accident at sea with one of our freighters and lost your sailboat. Is that correct?"

"Yes, it is. We are very lucky to be alive today. Our sailboat went down in 90 seconds after the *Hanjin Savannah* hit us. But we are very grateful to its crew who rescued us. However, since returning to the United States I have been shuffled from one person in your company to another, and I am prepared to sit here in this office today until someone will see or talk to us about our loss."

"Well, I'm also grateful that you survived the accident and that our people were able to assist in your rescue. I'm sorry that someone hasn't directed you to my office sooner. Would it be possible for you to fax a letter to me explaining everything about the accident and what has transpired so far?"

"Of course. We can do that right now and have this kind secretary fax it to you within the hour."

"After reviewing your letter, I will get back to you later today with the name of an agent who will handle your case."

Marshall thanked Mr. Barzin and hung up the phone. He turned to the secretary and asked her if there was somewhere we could type a letter and then have her fax it for us. She was very congenial and happy to accommodate our request. We sent the following letter.

Mr. Masoud Barzin
Claims Department
Hanjin Shipping Co. Ltd.
1521 Pier C Street
Long Beach, CA 90813
Dear Mr. Barzin:

Enclosed please find: (1) a copy of the Coast Guard report of the accident, (2) a brief summary of our account of the accident, and (3) a rough estimate of claim and property value lost (incomplete at this time due to outstanding medical bills, attorney fees, etc.).

We are of the belief that someone in Hanjin has initiated a file on our accident. Our belief stems from the following information:

a.   *Bae's name was given to us while we were aboard the* Hanjin Savannah.

b.   *Once home in the U.S., Bae referred us to Soon in your Long Beach office, indicating that he would be working with us on our claim.*

c.   *Marie Meadows, adjuster in San Francisco for Britannia Co., was hired by Hanjin to contact us and set up doctor appointments and later instructed us to forward medical bills to her.*

d.   *The American ambassador in Panama wrote to us that someone from Hanjin had contacted him in regard to our repatriation costs.*

e.   *The Coast Guard indicated to us that attorneys and surveyors hired by Hanjin had interviewed the crew from the* Hanjin Savannah *when they arrived in Georgia.*

Since our first contact with your company, two days after the collision, we have spoken with Bae and Soon on numerous occasions. Last Friday, April 16, Soon finally provided my husband with the name and phone number of a gentleman in Korea whom we were to contact and who supposedly would help us. He hung up on us because we didn't speak Korean.

Frustrated with the language barrier and the corporate shuffle, we stopped at the Seattle office and were put in contact with you.

We understand each company has its own policy as to how matters of this nature are handled, and our intent is not to offend Mr. Soon but hope that he accepts our apology. It is just that over one month has passed, and we know nothing more than the day of the accident. We are still homeless and waiting for someone to talk to. We're feeling frustrated, angry, and robbed of the life we have worked so hard to achieve. We are not looking for sympathy but hope that the Hanjin Company can see that we are real people put through the trauma of losing our home and almost our lives, and that it would treat us with more compassion than it would a damaged freight claim.

We look to you, Mr. Barzin, and your expert advice on how we can expedite these thoughts to the people in your company to settle this matter in a manner efficient and beneficial for both of us. We are most anxious to hear from you. You can contact us directly at 9xx-xxx-xxxx.

Sincerely,
Marshall and Dee Saunders

With the success rate we had had in the past with Hanjin personnel, we were dubious that we would hear anything back. But we were determined that we were not leaving that office until we got a response from someone. The secretary showed us to a lounge after we finished the letter and offered us coffee.

Once we were alone, Marshall looked at me and asked, "Well, do you want to make any bets on whether someone calls us back, or am I going to have to make a scene here today?"

"Oh, I have a feeling that today is going to be different. I think someone is going to get back to us," I answered.

Marshall doesn't like confrontations. He is the type of person who lights up a room when he enters. Always easygoing, he can put people at ease and make them laugh. His wit is quick and constant; he often startles me and everyone around him with his off-the-wall comments. He is the one who puts a smile on my face every morning.

However, when Marshall wants to make a point, he has an uncanny way of saying things directly to people that most others could never get away with. I never know what might come out of his mouth. He has the talent to make a definite point with humor without offending people.

The one thing Marshall isn't is patient. The word *patience* doesn't exist in his vocabulary, just as the word *no* didn't exist in our daughter Tiffany's vocabulary. I knew for certain that Marshall's patience had come to an end and we were not going to be leaving this office without being given the name of a person with whom we could negotiate. I wasn't sure how that was going to happen, but I knew Marshall would make it happen.

To pass the time we chatted about Marshall's brother. Craig's exploratory surgery had gone fine. Eventually he would need to have a new heart valve, but for now they were just monitoring his condition annually. Craig seemed sincerely happy that Marshall had come to be with him for the routine ordeal. And as I thought, it was good therapy for us, too. A lot of joking goes on between these two brothers, so even though we were dealing with tough issues, we enjoyed many good laughs those few days together.

Time passed fairly quickly in the lounge and sure enough, within a couple of hours the secretary entered the lounge and said that an insurance adjuster from Britannia in San Francisco was on the line. Marshall and I looked at each other in surprise, but we couldn't suppress our smiles.

Marshall talked with the adjuster. Her name was Marie Meadows and she was to represent Hanjin and work with us throughout the case. As it turned out, she was the same woman from Britannia who had called us shortly after we arrived home and had set up doctors' appointments for us. An appointment was set to meet with her in San Francisco late Friday morning.

We left the Hanjin office with an elated feeling and patting ourselves on the backs. This definitely was a good day, a positive step forward.

Before leaving Seattle we stopped to see Robert Perry, designer of our Tayana 52 who also designed hundreds of other popular sailboats. We were curious what other boats he could recommend that would perform similarly to the Tayana. We were looking for a boat with a modern hull underbody that would give us the same speed and performance but would be forgiving under most sea and weather conditions.

Not only did Bob give us some good suggestions to aid in the search for a new boat—such as to check out his newly designed Passport 50— he also gave excellent advice on how to negotiate with the South Korean shipping company. He had spent a lot of time in the Far East supervising production of many of his own designs, and had a fair amount of experience and knowledge of how negotiations work there.

Before we left his office, Bob advised, "Take the custom of saving face very seriously when negotiating with any of the people from Hanjin. Never back them in a corner; always leave them an out. Lay out your demands, and then ask for their advice or help. You will be amazed how much further you will get."

We thanked Bob for his advise and, and as we were leaving his office he yelled after us, "And check out the Passport 50."

We left Seattle with a new lift. The trip had been successful in all regards. We had delivered the paperwork to the insurance adjuster, and that seemed to go smoothly. He now had everything he needed to submit our claim to the main office in Florida. He was going to organize everything within the next day. Our visit with Craig and Linda was wonderful; we were so glad we were able to be there while he was in the hospital. We managed to walk the docks in Seattle and

Anacortes, and even look at the inside of a couple of boats that were advertised.

Best of all, we were going home with a scheduled appointment with someone representing Hanjin.

CHAPTER 19

The Puzzle Solved

IN THE MONTHS THAT FOLLOWED THERE WERE FOUR significant events that stood out. The first was receiving a check from our insurance company. There were many tense moments in the week prior to that happening. We had asked Debbie, our Florida adjuster, to send our paperwork to Gary, our lawyer. He would review everything before we signed final papers. These arrived, but Gary definitely was not happy with them. There were numerous phone calls back and forth between him, the insurance company, and us, over the rights of subrogation and our right to pursue Hanjin.

Lawrence, the insurer, was trying to prevent us from pursuing Hanjin for the rest of our claim. They had put a phrase in the final draft that gave only them the rights to pursue Hanjin. The rationale was that when we accepted a check for $160,000, they now owned the boat and had exclusive rights to pursue Hanjin for further claims. Our contention was that our insurance was only hull insurance, and we had a lot more invested and lost in personal items. The check would not even come close to covering our losses. We wanted to pursue our claim with Hanjin without Lawrence stepping in and interfering or taking the funds for which we were negotiating.

Gary, being the expert he was, immediately caught the phrase, worded very discreetly, that took away those rights. He came up with new wording. At first Lawrence said, "No way, the release form is the release form. This is our standard contract, take it or leave it. No one ever questions it."

A week elapsed with many tense phone calls between Gary, Lawrence, their attorneys, and us. At last Gary persevered and came up with new wording that allowed us to continue our negotiations with Hanjin without interference. Lawrence's legal counsel ultimately approved, but still maintained their subrogation rights clause that Debbie had told Marshall about on his first call to her.

Our check finally was issued at the end of April. Now at least we knew there were some funds available for a replacement boat. The amount we received was exactly $160,000 about one-third of the value of our boat and personal possessions. But it was a start and we were grateful.

It was just in time, too, for about three months later we heard that the insurance company had dissolved because of its many claims related to the hurricanes. The rumors we had heard turned out to be true. We were one of the lucky few who did get paid. The angel of luck was riding with us again.

The second event that stood out paramount in our minds in the aftermath of the accident occurred nearly two months later. We had picked up our mail at the Redding post office and were on our way down highway I-5 to meet with Gary, our attorney, and Marie, the Hanjin insurance adjuster. It was a long, boring drive, so I opened the mail along the way to pass the time. I noticed a letter from Gary. That was unusual because he generally called us with pertinent information.

The thickness of the envelope immediately aroused my curiosity. I slipped open the envelope and pulled out three depositions, two written in South Korean and one written in English. Gary explained in a letter that the Coast Guard had inspected the hull and bow-plainer for scratches on the *Savannah* and had boarded the ship and taken depositions from several of the crew when the ship docked in Georgia. Gary also forwarded copies of the depositions to us, and was working on getting a translation of the two written in Korean.

I started to scan the one in English. It read as if taken directly from the ship's log. It was from the man on watch the night of our accident, the pleasant young fellow who had come to our room to talk and then disappeared from our lives forever.

Mar. 15th 23:45	*I came on bridge for duty and confirmed ship's position, course, speed, and weather condition.*
Mar. 16th 00:00	*After undertaking the duty, I found that ship's Co. 123 degree, sp'd 19.3 k, wind sp'd 12k of North, weather fine but broken scattered clouds, sea moderate and vis. good (12-14 miles around). During the radar watch, I didn't find any obstructions on her route except the vessel on her aftward 8 miles off, which we have overtaken.*
Mar. 16th 00:15	*I confirmed no ships around by radar again and I didn't find any lights in sight during the continuous visual lookout.*
00:30	*Using the radar, I confirmed again that there were no obstructions on her route, and I also didn't find any lights by visual lookout continuously.*
00:44	*When keeping on watch, I sighted a flashing light on her port bow.*

"Marshall, they actually saw our light on their port side before the accident!"

> *Suddenly, I altered her course to stb'd with Helm Hard Stb'd and set the telegraph "Stop" position immediately.*

> 00:45 *I ordered A/O to call Master and I kept a sharp lookout around ship. But I couldn't find any lights and couldn't feel any collision.*

"Marshall . . . did you hear what I just read? This is incredible. Here in black and white are the answers to all our unsolved questions."

We had wondered why they insisted we were on their port side at the time of the collision. We knew we went down on the starboard side. Here, in black and white, the deposition explained it all. We already had been told that freight containers were stacked so high on the ship that the crew lost sight of anything within two miles of the bow. In the six minutes it took it to travel the two miles after they spotted us, we had crossed in front of its path. We originally were on 90-degree angles to each other. The man on watch thought we were still on his port side, where he had last seen us, and turned the ship hard to starboard and ran right over us.

Had Marie, Hanjin's insurance adjuster, seen a copy of this? We doubted it.

Our hunch was right. Half an hour later, as we sat across the desk from her, it was obvious this information was new to her.

Negotiations had been tedious and slow up to this point. We had pleaded continually that we were homeless and lost everything of value, and were looking to them to help make us whole again.

Hanjin finally released a check that covered our flight expenses home and our initial medical expenses. A few weeks later another check for $40,000 was released without any additional papers to sign. Gary was amazed at that. It was the company's gesture to cover some living expenses and to replace some basic items such as clothes.

We appreciated both checks and were prepared that it might be all that we would receive from Hanjin. However, we hoped for more and continued to negotiate with Marie. We wrote letters dramatizing how hard we had worked to achieve the dream of going off cruising in our own boat, and that now all that was gone. We provided her with long lists plus pictures borrowed from friends and family of the boat and all our possessions that were lost. We followed Robert Perry's advice, and ended each letter we sent or each session with Marie, by asking for advice on how we could come to an equitable agreement for all of us.

Armed with this new information, the situation had critically changed for us and for them—and the change definitely was in our favor. Here it was in black and white: The man on watch had altered course, and by so doing, had run over us. There was nothing Joe could have done to prevent the accident.

From that day on, negotiations moved fairly quickly. Events three and four occurred almost simultaneously.

Nicole, our youngest daughter, was graduating from college and we had gone to Sacramento to attend the ceremony and help her celebrate. It was at her graduation party that two important phone calls came in. One was for Nicole from the director of the health club, confirming her new job as head youth director of the brand-new facility. She would be in charge of setting up the entire youth program, including hiring a staff to help run it. We were very proud of her.

The second unexpected call was from Jim, our boat broker, who had been looking diligently for our replacement yacht.

"Hi, Marshall, it's Jim. I think I may have found a boat that will interest you."

"Really. What is it and where is it?" asked Marshall.

"It's in Seattle, and it's a Tatoosh 51 designed by Robert Perry. It was built in '85, but looks to be in excellent condition."

"When can we take a look at her?" Marshall asked excitedly.

"I've already put some pictures in the mail to you. If the timing works for you, I can get away next week. Why don't we plan on meeting in Seattle Tuesday to preview her?"

When the pictures arrived, *White Eagle* looked perfect for Marshall and me. We were excited; next Tuesday couldn't come soon enough. She was a 51-foot cutter — sleek, with a modern hull underbody, complete with a workshop for Marshall and a washer and dryer for me. We called Joe and told him the good news.

He was as excited as we were and asked, "If you buy the boat, can I join you in Seattle to look at it?"

"Of course, Joe. There will be lots to do, and we would love to have you join us."

"All right. Just let me know, and I'll be there ready to work on anything that needs to be done." We could tell by the tone of his voice that he was genuinely enthused and felt a sense of relief.

Marshall and I met Jim in Seattle. We stood on the upper dock looking down at

White Eagle. She was sleek, with a flush deck, and very appealing from that angle.

The moment we descended the companionway, Marshall and I exchanged glances. We were in love again. This was *our* boat.

I immediately walked over and stood behind the galley counter; it felt comfortable. Meanwhile, Marshall was checking out the engine room and the workshop.

She was a modern high-performance cutter with fin keel and supported-skeg rudder. She had a center cockpit, which gave us an incredible master stateroom.

After about two hours of poking into every nook and cranny, we asked Jim if it would be possible to arrange a preliminary sea trial. We knew this was unusual before an offer, but we were eager to see how she would sail.

Jim arranged it for later that day. In the light breeze, Marshall could tell immediately it was going to take some time to get used to driving from the center of the boat. Although visibility ahead was great, Marshall didn't feel he had as good a view of the jib for sail trim or as good a feel for how the boat was sailing. He was used to looking up the slot between the mainsail and the jib to trim the sails. This was definitely different, but he wasn't opposed to adjusting his old habits, and she did respond quickly in the light air, which was important to him.

We returned to the dock and had Jim write an offer contingent on a haulout and one more sea trial. We waited for a reply. The seller came back at full price. We were shocked and disappointed. The boat had been on the market for awhile, and we hoped he might be a little negotiable.

We were about to walk away from the transaction when the two boat brokers came up with the idea of a survey to be paid for by the seller. If the survey price came in at the asking price, would we agree to pay the full amount? We agreed, contingent on our check coming from Hanjin.

During this time we were trying to come to an agreement with Hanjin. The average current market value of a used Tayana was approximately $280,000. There were five on the market around the world. One was for sale in Long Beach for $285,000. Britannia had authorized us to make an offer of $280,000 on the used boat. Our offer was rejected when the sellers accepted another at full price. We were disappointed, but at least knew that Hanjin appeared to have agreed on a settlement that allowed us to get a boat of equal value to *Clambake*.

Their legal staff had drawn up some release papers that Gary was reviewing. They looked fine except for the fact that we were not indemnified from Lawrence if Lawrence pressed for their subrogation rights. The legal force for Britannia was from London, and British law was not familiar with subrogation rights. Basically these gave Lawrence rights to the first $160,000, the amount of our insurance, in the event we received any money for the accident from Hanjin.

Gary and Britannia went back and forth about the indemnifying clause for about a week. Again, Gary prevailed and came up with wording that allowed us to accept an amount from Hanjin for a combined total of $200,000. If Lawrence pursued their rights under the subrogation clause, then Hanjin would additionally pay Lawrence $120,000. As it turned out, Lawrence never pursued their rights, even though Gary sent them a letter advising them what we had negotiated.

We signed the final paperwork before we left for Seattle, and again, Lady Luck was with us. We received a check from Hanjin the same day that we came to a mutual agreement with the seller of our new boat. On June 15th, only 90 days after our accident, we were living aboard our new home, *White Eagle*.

Although we had been incredibly lucky to accomplish all of this within 90 days, we felt it was because we had diligently pursued our goal every single day. We delivered every piece of paperwork in person and immediately followed through with phone calls and confirmation letters. There was not one day during this period that we didn't devote at least an hour or two—and some days a lot more—to our goal of returning to our cruising lifestyle or to searching for a new boat.

We took time out to look at boats on each trip we made to meet with our attorney in San Francisco. We had searched every harbor on the West Coast from San Diego to Seattle and spent hours poring over magazines advertising boats for sale. We probably were aware of and looked at every boat available on the Pacific Coast over that three-month period. We knew if she were out there, we would find her. *White Eagle* was our destiny. She came soaring into our lives just when we needed her most.

CHAPTER 20

Facing the Future

Washington law mandates that a newly purchased boat be moved out of the state within 45 days or the owner is required to pay state sales tax. So after provisioning White *Eagle* with new electronics and spiffing her up with Joe's help, we again headed down the coast to San Francisco where we decided to have the christening party.

We invited everyone, including Gary, our attorney, and Marie, the adjuster from Britannia. All were amazed at what we had been able to accomplish in such a short time.

A couple of friends couldn't resist telling us, "We're shocked that you would want to return to the cruising lifestyle. Aren't you a little concerned about going back out there again?"

"Not really. It would be like saying I'll never drive a car again after being in an auto accident," Marshall retorted.

Our children and family knew we would return to the cruising lifestyle, but they kept silent even though they inwardly hoped we wouldn't after giving them such a scare.

Gary, our attorney, was simply in awe. He repeated over and over, "I amazed at what you kids accomplished in 90 days. I've never seen the likes of it in an international case. It's an absolute first, and I would have bet big dollars against your ever accomplishing what you did. I think I need to hire the two of you onto my staff."

We laughed and thanked him for his invaluable help, but told him, "No, thanks; legal work isn't exactly what we have in mind for the next couple of years."

Dean, our ham contact in Santa Cruz, was eager to see us back out there. We talked with him daily on the radio, and he wanted to know the details of every new adventure. He lived our trip vicariously through the radio, in return keeping us in contact via phone patches with all of our family. He knew before we did when Sheri was pregnant with our first grandchild, and that Lisa was given an engagement ring. He was the bearer of good news, bad news, and sad news. He was our tie to our folks and children for nine long years and had become a big part of our family.

During the party, everyone had some words of wisdom to pass on. Although Marshall's grandmother wasn't able to attend, her suggestion was my favorite.

We had driven down to visit her in Sun City, California, before we took off for Mexico. We were sitting in her cozy apartment living room telling her about our new boat and our plans to continue with our dream. She was very sharp and looked incredible for 96. She was taking notes on a little pad and asking lots of questions.

Finally, she laid her pen in her lap and looked over at us, shaking her head. "Oh dears, I wish you would reconsider after all you have been through. Don't you think it would be wiser to invest in a farm? Maybe buy a cow or two?"

Marshall couldn't resist teasing her, "But Nana, cows don't float."

"Sonny, you have your grandfather's and great-grandfather's genes. They were boat people, too."

We were back on the cow—or horse, so to speak—but the big question loomed out there: where do we go? We had discussed this issue quite a few times in the past, but there was never an urgency to make a decision, for at that time we didn't own a boat. Now our new home was reality and we had to decide. The accident had let the air out of our sails, but deep in our souls we knew we wanted to continue with our dream. We had been concentrating so hard on *returning* to our cruising lifestyle that we didn't take time to think about where we would go this time.

We decided to head south to Mexico again and see how we felt after we arrived there. We knew the anchorages and the drill for checking in and out of all the towns with Customs, Immigration, and the port captains. It would give us time to regroup and regain our enthusiasm to relax and enjoy the cruising lifestyle again.

But it was Nana who inspired us. She was born in the Turks Islands and was a poor, but beautiful conch girl. She married into a wealthy family from Nassau and shortly after, gave birth to Marshall's father. Her husband ran the mail route on an old schooner between the Bahamas and Miami, and occasionally ran a little rum during Prohibition. The family never approved of the marriage, so when Marshall's dad was only a baby, Nana ran off to Miami and raised him on her own.

She often told us tales of the Bahamas and that she dreamed of returning one day to the place where she was born. In fact it was her idea to meet us there to celebrate her 100th birthday on our boat. (She almost made it, but died three weeks before her birthday. But she knew that her grandson had made it there for her.)

On the way back to our boat with Nana as our inspiration, we decided the Turks Islands in the Bahamas should become our new goal and destination.

"But this time we are taking along a big eraser. If it doesn't feel right, we change directions," Marshall suggested.

"Sounds good to me," I said, flashing him a big smile.

In a matter of weeks we were heading south for the second time in three years. No fears, no apprehensions clouded our minds or the joy we felt. Relief that we had been able to resolve our problems in such a short time without going to court permeated our hearts and souls.

It was great to be back doing what we had worked our whole lives to do. We were out there again, living our dream. Neither of us was sure where we would wind up this time, but we knew we had made the right decision. It felt wonderful not having to deal with bureaucracy, insurance companies, and big corporations on a daily basis. Of course, we had no control over Mother Nature, but all the other problems were ours and could be solved by us alone. There was something very comforting in the fact that once again we were at the helm and in control of our lives. As always, destiny would be our guide.

CHAPTER 21

The EPIRB Issue

HERE STILL WAS ONE UNRESOLVED ISSUE. WHY HADN'T THE Coast Guard received a signal from our brand new EPIRB? Was it a fluke, or should we be concerned for the safety of the five other cruisers who also purchased them new in Puerto Vallarta just before we were ready to make the South Pacific crossing? All of the other boats had left for ports unknown. I felt an obligation to let them know that our unit had not worked. Perhaps theirs might have a problem, also.

I decided to write a factual letter to *Latitude 38,* a favorite magazine read by most of the cruising community. Even in the middle of nowhere, cruisers seem to figure out ways to have relatives send them the latest issues. I believed this publication had the best chance of getting this information to our cruising friends who already had made the ocean crossing and were in ports scattered across the Pacific.

The EPIRB had been sent in late March to the Coast Guard in Alameda. The Coast Guard called the manufacturer to say that they would be testing it and that they believed there was a problem with the unit. During that conversation the manufacturer suggested to the Coast Guard that they it might be more capable of testing it, with their specialized equipment. So unknown to us, the EPIRB was forwarded to the manufacturer.

While we were in the midst of filing depositions with the insurance company and trying to track down someone from Hanjin to talk with us, we received a phone call from a man at the EPIRB manufacturing company.

"Hello! I'm John Mitchell from _____ Industries. The Coast Guard has sent us your EPIRB. We've got it here and I'll be working on it. We will be thoroughly testing it and get to the bottom of this. Can you give me a brief explanation of when the EPIRB was turned on and how long you had it activated?"

Marshall told him, "We turned it on prior to abandoning ship and didn't turn it off until we were in the hospital room aboard the freighter. To the best of my recollection, it had to be close to a couple of hours."

Mitchell then asked Marshall, "What are your expectations from our company?"

"I have none. I gave it to the Coast Guard to see if they could figure out what went wrong so the same thing doesn't happen to other cruisers."

"Okay, good. If you have any further questions, don't hesitate to call. We'll be working on it to figure out what went wrong. We'll get to the bottom of this. Let me give you my 800 number. Feel free to call if you have any questions."

Marshall wrote down his name and number, thanked him, and hung up.

"That was a strange call," he frowned.

"Why, who was it?" I asked.

"It was a man from _____ Industries. Said he had our EPIRB there and he was going to test it. Strange the Coast Guard didn't let us know they were sending it to the manufacturer. I feel a little funny about that."

"Yeah, that is a little strange. Who was the man who called?"

"He said his name was John Mitchell. Sounded like a technician behind a bench. He told me they were going to test it and send the findings to the Coast Guard. I guess the Coast Guard will let us know what is going on eventually."

The call came at a time when we were knee-deep in alligators with other more important issues, and so this had gone to the bottom of the list. But I made sure the man's name and number was entered in our daily log.

About two weeks after Mitchell's call, the Coast Guard called to say that the manufacturer had returned the EPIRB with a note that the unit was working according to manufacturer's specs. The note suggested that perhaps the problem was with the operation, not the performance. It insinuated that the owners, in the confusion of the accident, might never have turned it on or left it on long enough for a satellite to pass over and pick up the signal.

The gentleman from the Coast Guard also was a little perplexed by the response and got permission from NOAA, the National Oceanic and Atmospheric Administration, to set off the signal and test it. It worked. We questioned the Coast Guard to determine if it was possible the satellite didn't receive our signal from the unit. The officer told me to call NOAA and ask that question.

The person I spoke with at NOAA asked me to write a letter giving him our latitude and longitude and time and date when we had the EPIRB activated. He would research if any satellites had passed over us.

We knew the time and date and had confirmed the exact position with the ship's captain. The EPIRB had been activated when Marshall handed it to Joe while still aboard *Clambake*. The strobe light was blinking. We never turned it off until after we were aboard the freighter and in the infirmary one and one-half hours later.

Within a couple of weeks, we received a letter from NOAA telling us that one satellite had passed over us during that period. The man from NOAA indicated that if our EPIRB was activated and working, a signal should have been received and transmission sent to the tracking station.

UNITED STATES DEPARTMENT OF COMMERCE
National Oceanic and Atmospheric Administration
NATIONAL ENVIRONMENTAL SATELLITE, DATA,
AND INFORMATION SERVICE
Washington, D.C. 20233

November 26, 1993   E/SP3:AM

Mr. and Mrs. Marshall Saunders
P.O. Box 493930
Redding, CA 96049

Dear Mr. and Mrs. Saunders:

    In response to your letter dated October 27, 1993, we have inspected our data for any beacon signals from your 406 MHz EPIRB. The identifier you have provided us (AO-587) is not used by our system. An inquiry into our 406 Registration Database provided us with the information listed below to help conduct our search. Please verify that the information is correct.

- Owner: Marshall E Saunders
- EPIRB ID: ADCE0146CC40801
- Vessel: White Eagle
- Registration: 652730

    The results, using the EPIRB ID listed above, indicate that our system did not receive any signals from your 406 MHz EPIRB on or around March 16, 1993. During the time that you indicated your EPIRB was active (00:45-02:15 local), a satellite did pass over your location at 01:55 local. A search of any signals from the 121.5 MHz homer on your EPIRB also was negative.

Sincerely,

William C. Burkhart

William C. Burkhart
SARSAT Operations Manager

Now there still was the looming question of why the Coast Guard hadn't received any such signal. Because of this concern I felt compelled to write the factual letter to the magazine *Latitude 38*.

The day I was about to mail it, Marshall suggested, "Do you think we should send the manufacturing company a copy of your letter and give them a chance to respond? I still have the 800 number the technician gave me that day."

"I think that's a great idea!" I replied.

Later that afternoon, from the Ballena Bay Marina near Alameda, I dialed the number and got a friendly operator from the manufacturing company. I asked to speak to John Mitchell. She kindly responded that John Mitchell was not available at this number, but he was their corporate attorney and she would be happy to give me "his" number. I explained to her the reason for my call and decided to just leave a message for her to pass on to whomever she felt appropriate to respond.

I couldn't wait to get off the phone and tell Marshall what I had just found out. The man whom we thought was a technician behind a bench examining our EPIRB was the corporate attorney. He had never identified himself as such.

"Leaves a few more questions to be answered, doesn't it?" I exclaimed to Marshall. "And what a coincidence, with the name John Mitchell. I'm sure it couldn't possibly be the same John Mitchell who was attorney general of the U.S. and later served jail time for perjury during Watergate. Naah, has to just be a fluke."

Marshall sat there rubbing his cheek. "I wonder what he was thinking when we called? Sounds to me like he was trying to weigh where we were coming from."

We decided to send our letter to *Latitude* that afternoon and not wait for a response from the EPIRB company, but out of courtesy, I first faxed _____Industries a copy of the letter. Within a day, we received several phone messages from the manufacturer asking us to have our attorney get in touch with their legal counsel ASAP. The message cautioned us against a possible charge of inflammatory assault if the article were published.

Our intent from the beginning was never to sue the manufacturer, but only to find out why our EPIRB did not work and to warn other cruisers to have their units checked. The manufacturer assumed the worst and used threats to intimidate us. We sent the letter to *Latitude*.

The letter was published in the next issue, but not before I had had several interesting conversations with several of the manufacturer's executives. This occurred while we were traveling south in our new boat, *White Eagle*. A trail of messages followed us down the coast, left with everybody we knew, including our daughter, Sheri, and the Coast Guard.

When we reached San Diego and checked with Sheri, she gave us the urgent message that one of the VPs of the company needed to talk to me.

I dialed the number from the marina phone booth.

"Hi, I'm Dee Saunders and was given the message to call you."

"Yes, thank you for calling. We are concerned at some of your insinuations in the article to *Latitude*."

"I felt I was being quite factual," I responded.

"Yes, well you referred to the unit as being a life-saving device. This unit was merely designed to send a signal to a satellite. You could be liable for defamation of the product."

"I see. You are the vice-president; please explain to me then why I should buy one of your units. If it's not a life-saving device, exactly what is it designed for? Even your magazine ads refer to it in that manner. Give me your sales pitch. Why should I spend $1,200 to buy your EPIRB if it's not meant to save my life? Just what should I expect it to do for me?"

"Well . . . it was designed to send out a series of beeps per second that a satellite will pick up as it passes over the unit."

"Yes, and then what? What else does it do?"

"That's all it was designed for. It sends the series of beeps that the satellite forwards to a NOAA receiving station. Those are government controlled. We have no authority over any of that portion of the relay."

"I see. So I paid $1,200 for a box that sends out a beep that may or may not be received."

"That's correct. We have no control over the satellites or the user and how long he keeps the EPIRB operational."

"Well, tell me this. Do you have any idea why our signal was not received by the satellite if we definitely know that a satellite passed over us during its operation?"

"I really don't. We have sold thousands of units and have never had a complaint like this before."

"Really! Think about what you just said. Kind of sounds like the same answer a parachute manufacturer would give when a chute didn't open."

"I guess you have a point. I do have to admit, it appears something went wrong. I'm not sure what it was."

The conversation ended shortly after that remark. I couldn't wait to get back to the boat and tell Marshall what just transpired. Oh, how I wished I had had a tape.

The company finally did respond with a letter to *Latitude* that had strong negative innuendos about the way we used the EPIRB and also implied that our surmise that they may have fixed the unit was entirely false.

We never did resolve the "why," although we had our suspicions. We decided not to waste any more negative energy pursuing it, for I had accomplished part of what I wanted—to warn other cruisers not to rely on an EPIRB working. It was time to focus on where we were going, on enjoying our new home, and on embracing our second chance to be out there cruising.

CHAPTER 22

Return to the Dream

After leaving the California coast, it didn't take us long to fall back into the rhythm of cruising. The air soon turned warm and balmy and daylight hours grew longer as we traveled farther south. Life again was good and dealing with the aftermath of our accident—daily phone calls to our insurance company and Hanjin—soon became only a memory. Being back on the water and living on the boat felt comfortable. It was fun to restart our journey back in a country where we knew the good anchorages, the customs and language of the people, and the paperwork procedures involved with the check-ins at each new port of call.

However, as we continued down the coast of Baja I noticed a slight change in Marshall. He seemed more intense, especially when any mechanical problem arose. It appeared to me that he was beginning to treat each problem as if it were an emergency.

This was not at all like Marshall. Normally he was a calm, humorous, and communicative person. When problems arose in the past, he always had a way of letting me know the severity of the problem but at the same time putting me at ease.

He tried to let me know if it was solvable or fixable. But he definitely was acting differently this trip.

He would start out calmly proclaiming, "Something seems to be wrong with the steering."

Immediately the intensity would increase.

"Dee, this is a problem. I need your help immediately." His voice was now a lot more forceful.

"Okay, what do you need me to do?" I would ask.

"Here, take over the helm," he would order and then disappear into the depths of the engine room.

I would drive the boat, patiently waiting for some word from Marshall as to what the emergency was. My heart would start to beat faster and a knot would develop in my stomach. I would continue to try to be patient, but it was difficult not knowing what was going on below. But Marshall wasn't talking.

Finally my apprehensions would build to a point that my body would start to tremble and I couldn't be patient any longer. I would yell to him, "What is the problem, Marshall?"

He would snap back, "I don't know."

I would go back to driving the boat and waiting, but my worries would build. Thoughts would run rampant. "*Is there a leak? Are we sinking?*"

The hard part was not having any idea what the problem was or how much of an emergency it was. Marshall wasn't giving me any information and this wasn't like him. He normally was calm, cool, and collected when any problem arose on the boat. In the past he had always gone to great efforts to put my mind at ease assuring me the problem was solvable.

This scenario began happening more frequently and it usually turned out to be a minor problem. Don't get me wrong, I'm very appreciative of Marshall's mechanical talents and I think he is incredibly brilliant and gifted. I don't think there is anything on the boat he can't eventually figure out how to fix. It always amazes me that he has so much mechanical sense and knowledge, including the uncanny ability to figure out how to make things work with the limited supplies available in the middle of nowhere. However, I knew I couldn't continue to handle the roller coaster of emotions that accompanied these episodes. If this was how our ocean cruising was going to be, I was ready to give it up. I wasn't sleeping very well, especially under way. I found I needed to sleep in the cockpit instead of down below to get any sleep at all. When I tried sleeping below, images of the night of the accident returned. I felt trapped.

Finally, I decided we needed to talk, and we did.

I started out explaining, "Marshall, I can't handle that every time there is a problem with the boat I get the feeling from you that it is an emergency. You disappear below and don't give me any clue as to what the emergency is. I'm up here driving the boat wondering, are we going to sink? Do I need to deploy the life raft, or radio a Mayday? I need to know something," I pleaded.

Marshall responded defensively, "But I don't know right away what the problem is. It takes me awhile to figure out what's wrong and how to fix it."

"Yes, I understand that; but generally you can tell immediately if it's a life-and-death situation—if we're sinking. That's what I need to know. I'm here at the helm and have no clue what is going on in the engine room. I don't expect or need to know the exact problem or how you are going to fix it; I just need to know that it's not another *Clambake* situation, okay?"

"Okay, I'll try and let you know something. It's just that when there is a problem I like to solve it right away if I can, before it develops into something worse where we have an even bigger problem—and besides, you don't say anything, so I figure you don't have any interest in what the problem is."

"You're totally wrong. I care very much," I explained. "My stomach is in knots up here, but I choose to remain quiet allowing you to think things out clearly without interruption. Believe me, I am concerned—my mind is conjuring up all sorts of scenarios of what else could go wrong while you are down there working. I don't think you realize it, but you snap at me when I ask you a question when you are under pressure trying to figure out what is wrong."

Marshall had no idea what I was talking about, and I could tell from his defensive answer that he wasn't even aware of what he was doing.

The situation repeated itself a few more times, but with some gentle reminders (such as an explosive "I can't handle this anymore!") the panic on my part and emergencies on Marshall's began to come less frequently and finally faded into a thing of the past, as did the memories of *Clambake*.

We began to relax and fall back into our cruising routine of having fun and taking each day and problem one at a time. Life again was good. I was sleeping better and Marshall was back to communicating with me when problems arose.

We followed our former route down the Baja coast into the Sea of Cortez, revisiting all of our favorite places—La Paz, Puerto Escondido, Aqua Verde, Mulege, and Bahía Concepción. As Christmas approached we crossed the Sea of Cortez and headed down the mainland. Marshall and I discussed inviting Joe to join us as we rounded Cabo Corrientes off Puerto Vallarta. That was the last point on shore we passed before our fatal accident. Unfortunately, work prevented him from joining us this time, but he jumped at the opportunity to meet us in Huatulco and do the leg to Costa Rica later.

CHAPTER 23

The Freeze-Dried Peas

TWO YEARS AFTER THE ACCIDENT WE WERE IN BARRA DE Navidad, a picturesque fishing village nestled at the back of Melaque Bay on the west coast of Mexico, enjoying a wonderful Christmas dinner with fellow cruisers. Eight of us were down below squeezed around the cozy dining table on our newly refurbished *White Eagle*. We were enjoying turkey, dressing, and all the trimmings of a Christmas feast. Prior to that day, we had decided to share in a gift exchange of white elephant presents to conclude the festivities.

Marshall and I searched the boat for an appropriate gift and came across the package of freeze-dried peas that had survived the accident. We went to the computer and made up a little outline showing the history and life of this package. It went something like this:

1975: Purchased in Hawaii.

1976: Traveled to Tahiti, Tuamotus, Marquesas, and back to Hawaii.

1978: Traveled Hawaii to California.

1979: Remained in safe storage in California garage until 1991.

1991:   Traveled from British Columbia to
         Mexico.
1992:   Survived Hurricane Lester, Santa Rosalia.
1993:   March 16, sunk at sea off coast of Mexico,
         but survived.
1993:   March 22, subject of mugging in Miami,
         but survived.
1993   July, British Columbia to Mexico, again.

A couple about to return home and sell their boat drew the gift. They were superstitious, and so, unknown to us, threw the package of peas overboard. Other friends who had purchased a house on the canal in the area retrieved the peas a couple of days later. They found the package washed ashore on the beach by their home and recognized it from the Christmas party.

The only reason I mention this is that shortly after returning home that spring we received a package in the mail. There was no letter or explanation. The sole contents were our famed freeze-dried peas, with a new outline of its life to date:

1995   Christmas—Given to a new owner
         (*Interlude*, Ken and Carol).
1995   December 26—Thrown overboard and
         Interlude exorcised.
1995   December 27—Washed ashore at Casita
         Hiolani in Barra de Navidad.
1996   Survived an earthquake and numerous
         aftershocks in damaged garage at home on
         the canal in Barra de Navidad.
1996   Survived the Rat from Hell who ate
         through *Hiolani*'s (our catamaran) survival
         bag, including the space blankets, all the
         food and water, but didn't eat the peas.
1996   June 24—Survived Hurricane Alma.

1996   June 25—Sent on journey back to original
owners (we pray that God blesses all deliv-
ery personnel involved).

This was our new good-luck omen. The peas had survived everything. They had traveled with Marshall through the
South Seas, endured hurricanes, earthquakes, and the sinking
of *Clambake*. They had been thrown away into the sea and still

White Eagle *moored in Port Escondido, Mexico.*

Exchanging famed freeze-dried peas during Christmas dinner with fellow cruisers aboard White Eagle *in Barre de Navidad, Mexico.*

found their way back to us. Surely this must be a positive sign.

We had spent two wonderful years in Mexico and it was time to begin our travels south. We made new plans. When we left the Washington coast I had promised Marshall I would go any direction with him in our new boat as long as we didn't go over the same spot where our beloved *Clambake* was resting. As Marshall and I discussed various possibilities, we agreed our goal still was Nana's birthplace, the Turks Islands.

It was time to call Joe and arrange for him to join us. However, his arrival would have to be scheduled about one month out. Before leaving Mexico we had promised my parents a two-week vacation on the boat. We had arranged previously that they would meet us in Ixtapa, and that was only a week away.

Marshall called Joe, who sounded excited about the prospect of joining us later that month. He indicated he would have no problem arranging to be off work. His plans for heading south were set in motion.

CHAPTER 24

Death Aboard
White Eagle

THIS CHAPTER IS ABOUT MY MOTHER'S DEATH ON OUR boat in Ixtapa, Mexico. Don't skip it or turn to the next chapter—it's not sad or depressing; it was good. At least as good as a death aboard a boat can possibly be . . . and if you have done any cruising in a foreign country and gone through check-in procedures with Immigration and Customs, you can begin to draw a mental picture of what possibly could have been involved.

Let's talk about mother. She was a real beauty in her early days—a redhead, a Susan Sarandon type with a fiery, outgoing personality—but as a mother she was a strong-willed woman and strict disciplinarian, almost puritanical and Victorian in her beliefs. She was not the kind of mother you loved. I loved her because she was my mother, but I was not close to her. I respected her, feared her, and many times cursed her under my breath. She was relentless in her discipline and expected perfection of my sister and me.

I recall a fairly recent conversation with my sister where we tried reminiscing about our childhood. It was strange that neither of us could remember much about our early years or much interaction with mother. We remembered coming home from school to an empty house—mother worked at the local department store—and doing our chores and homework. We remembered going to church every Sunday. We remembered our annual family trip to Ocean City, New Jersey, and the weeks spent on the beach. We recalled the annual family clambake with aunts, uncles and cousins . . . and we remembered the discipline. Mother was strong, determined, and relentless. I still can close my eyes and hear her say, "Wipe that smirk off your face . . . don't you dare use that tone with me . . . I don't want to hear you say you can't do it; I don't ever want to hear you say that again. You *can* do it if you try."

I now appreciate and give total credit to my mother for one of my strongest adult personality traits. I acquired the trait through her constant harping and repetition of the words, "You can do it." And then there was the little song she sang, "You can do it, you can do it, if you try." It wasn't until I began writing this book that I realized what a gift my mother had given me by repeating those words to me thousands of times.

From early childhood she had instilled in me the belief that I could do anything if I tried. She had instilled it to the degree that it became ingrained and second nature, as natural as brushing my teeth before I went to bed. To this day, it never crosses my mind that I can't do something; I just assume I can, and find a way to accomplish it.

When I think of mother in my adult years, I remember her as a negative person. I never remember her telling me that something looked nice, or someone did something well, or that she liked something someone else was doing. In fact, from my viewpoint, she appeared to dwell on looking for the negative in other people or in my family and me. I never felt rancor or bitterness toward her when she expressed her negative opinions, but in reaction to her critical nature, I tended to focus on the positive. I always dreaded her visits to our home because it was during these visits that she especially focused her negative verbal opinions on my family.

She did have her good side and gave to us in her way. She enjoyed knitting, so every year she would knit sweaters, mittens, or hats for the entire family for Christmas. I can't even begin to imagine the time she devoted to making these gifts, because as time went on there were 17 of us in our extended families. That was her true show of love.

I am grateful that our last few days together were such good ones.

Mother had been sick for more than a year. Suffering from heart failure, she was taking medications prescribed by her doctor. She had lost a lot of weight and I knew her situation was fragile. I spoke to her via ham radio frequently and although she never complained about her illness, which was one other thing I admired about her, I knew she was uncomfortable and ailing and her time was drawing near. I had spoken to my sister several times questioning her about Mother's condition and if she thought I should make a special trip home. Mother and dad were scheduled to join us for two weeks in Zihautenejo in March. I had made reservations at a hotel on the beach because mother had to sleep in a reclining position, her head elevated. She loved being on the boat, but I thought she might be more comfortable in a real bed propped with pillows, as opposed to a bunk on a sailboat.

"No, don't make a special trip up. Mother will make it down there," my sister assured me. She wants to see you on the boat."

As much as she criticized so many things about our life, I knew mother did enjoy her trips on our boat. What also amazed me is that she encouraged Marshall and me to travel. She never discouraged us from venturing across the ocean—not even after our accident. She knew it was our goal and perhaps in a way she was able to see the fulfillment of her lectures: "You can do it if you try."

March arrived and so did mother and dad. When I first saw mother as she got off the plane, my heart sank. She was skin and bones and almost meek looking. I had no idea she had gotten that bad. The first few days mother and dad stayed in the hotel on the beach and we anchored *White Eagle* right in front to be close by. But it wasn't long before mother insisted on moving onto the boat. We decided anchoring out would be difficult for her, so we moved to the pleasant modern marina at the adjoining town of Ixtapa. This allowed mother easier access on and off the boat and it also allowed us the use of the beautiful oceanside pool and gave her the opportunity to do a little walking.

Two weeks flew by as we spent our days taking leisurely walks to the pool area, where the four of us would spend the afternoon playing Pinochle, interspersed with dips in the pool to cool off. Mother would take a few sidestrokes to the prompt of my cheers and encouragement. She admitted this was the best she had felt in days.

Marshall even encouraged her to "belly up" to the pool bar and have a margarita. At first she begrudgingly balked at the idea, but with some more encouragement she finally took a seat at the pool bar. We detected a slight grin as we got her to hold up her drink while posing on the underwater bar stool for a photo with dad.

That time spent together was quality. It was probably the first time in my life that a visit with mother went really well.

When we had spent that much time together in the past, we normally ended up arguing. She would find something negative about our life to dwell on, usually how liberally we raised our children. Eventually I would have enough of her lectures or criticism, and as much as I would try to hold my tongue, I would explode and we would come to words. It didn't happen on this trip and I am so grateful. Maybe I was more tolerant of her jibes because she was ailing, or maybe there were fewer jibes *because* of her ailing.

The day before mom and dad were to depart was perfect. We spent the afternoon at the pool overlooking the ocean. Mother and I defeated dad and Marshall at Pinochle. She had built up her endurance over the two weeks so she was able to take 16 side-strokes in the pool, to my cheers and praise. She said she couldn't believe how well she was feeling and sleeping at night.

That evening we had a wonderful dinner at a quaint Italian dinner house overlooking the marina, after which we went back to the boat to play one more game of Pinochle. Mother and I had an incredible hand and wiped out the men.

She went to bed and never woke up.

The following morning dad came calling for Marshall at our stateroom door.

"Marshall—Marshall, I think there is a problem with Altheda. I can't get her to wake up," his voice quivered.

Marshall jumped out of bed and went to mother's stateroom to check. I followed close behind. Mother was in the forward double bunk lying on her back with a sheet pulled up around her shoulders. She had a peaceful expression on her face.

Marshall took her wrist and felt for a pulse, but there did not appear to be any. She was cold and did not seem to be breathing. I kept pressing my ear to her mouth, listening for the slightest sound of a breath. I was hoping to hear something, but seeing her stillness, I knew I wouldn't.

Altheda relaxing in the pool.

She had died peacefully in her sleep without a sound.

Mother and dad were supposed to fly out that morning, but I swear Mother knew in her mind how *she* was going to do this. She had seen my sister and her husband, all the grandchildren and their families, and she was at peace knowing all of *us* were okay. She was free to drift peacefully into the night, knowing I was there to help dad through this.

The next few hours aboard our boat were a blur. We called a doctor to verify her death, and then every official in Ixtapa and Zihautenejo came aboard to observe the situation before they would remove her body. Initially, they had to treat it as a crime scene.

After several hours one of the officials, possibly the doctor, contacted a funeral parlor to make arrangements to remove her body.

Later that day, my father was required to go to the police station for an interrogation. I accompanied him, but they would not allow me in the interrogation room with him. They did allow a translator from the American Embassy to accompany him, for which I was grateful. I was allowed to remain outside the room and could call in to him from time to time to be sure he was okay. I felt terrible that he had to go through this on top of losing his wife, but he surprised me with his strength.

The following morning we had an appointment at the funeral parlor. My mother's wishes were to be cremated, but the closest crematorium was in Acapulco. We were informed that we had to purchase a casket to ship her body to Acapulco—it was some government requirement or some local funeral parlor's scheme to make money, we never were sure which.

At first the funeral parlor wanted to charge us more than $1,000 for the casket, but we were able to barter for one for less than half that amount after Marshall threatened to put her in a suitcase and drive her to Acapulco himself.

We also had to deal with authorities on the issue of an autopsy. Mother would have been against one and so was dad, but the authorities were insistent. Marshall finally was able to bribe the doctor for about $400. He agreed to sign a statement saying that mother was under his care and taking medications for heart failure. This appeared to satisfy the officials and be sufficient to waive the autopsy. This is one of the many reasons I love Mexico: Money can almost always make things happen.

The owners of the funeral parlor told us that the cremation process and paperwork would take about a week. During that time we made arrangements with the airlines so I could accompany dad home, using mother's ticket.

The day came to leave for Pennsylvania. We had stopped by the funeral parlor the afternoon before, where dad was presented with the official death certificate and a beautiful box decorated with Mexican tiles holding Mother's ashes. I already had decided that I was not going to pack the ashes and risk our luggage being lost in a foreign country. Mother was going to travel with me.

We checked in at the American Airlines counter at the Itaxpa airport where I handed the young man at the counter Dad's tickets, our passports, and the official copy of mother's death certificate.

"Where is your mother?" asked the polite young man behind the counter.

I set the box on the counter and pointed to it.

The reaction was priceless. I have never understood how the Mexican people view death, but I know it involves a combination of humor, superstition, and reverence. With flailing arms and lots of muttering, the flustered young man ushered my father and me through the line. I chuckled to myself and would have loved to know what he was thinking. I had a feeling he was afraid I might offer to show him what was in the box.

The same reaction occurred again at the security check station and then again in Mexico City, where we transferred planes.

We made it home to Pennsylvania without any mishaps. Ironically, my sister's flight from California intersected with ours in Chicago and she flew the last leg of the flight home with us. I was so glad to see her and I was grateful we were able to be there to help dad through this. I felt badly that he had to deal with the extra bureaucracy problems of being in a foreign country, in addition to the emotions of handling mother's death.

I was sorry that my mother's life was over, but I did not feel sadness. I felt badly but without grief or guilt. I don't think my sister or father felt sadness, either. We never talked about it, but none of us shed a lot of tears. We had a nice memorial service for mother and I know she is in heaven still creating some havoc and guiding us through life.

My sister swears it was "mother," that was on her roof during the night of a terrible recent windstorm, flinging the roof shingles as far as she could throw them. They found some a couple of blocks away. My sister did wind up with a badly needed new roof after the storm, thanks to the many missing tiles, the insurance company—and maybe mother.

After mother's death, dad started talking. I guess he never had a chance when she was alive. She always dominated conversations and never let anyone else get a word in. We never knew dad had so much to say, and we learned a lot about his life that we had not known.

As for me, it has taken many adult years to figure out what mother was about. I'm still not sure I really know, but I realize she gave me some special gifts. The most important one was the power to believe in myself and know that I can do anything if I try. I'm sorry she is not here for me to thank her . . . but somehow I think she knows.

CHAPTER 25

Joe

TWO WEEKS LATER, JOE ARRIVED IN HUALTUCO ON SCHEDule, all smiles and excited to accompany us on the leg to Costa Rica.

"All set for another adventure?" Marshall asked.

"You bet, and hey, I don't want you guys to worry about night watches." Joe grinned sheepishly. "You can be sure I will be the best *watch person* you can ever find."

I hugged Joe and said, "We already knew that."

But lo and behold, as Murphy's Law would have it, Joe had another heart-stopper his first night on watch.

We left Huatulco traversing the Gulf of Tehuantepec heading for Guatemala. It was Joe's first night on watch and there was an incredible amount of phosphorescence in the water, a phenomenon Joe had never experienced. Marshall and I retired below, leaving Joe on watch at the helm. We immediately drifted off into a deep sleep, knowing *White Eagle* was in good hands.

It wasn't long before we were startled awake by a loud "Holy shit!"

Anxious, expecting the worse, Marshall went flying topside to see what was happening.

Joe bargaining in Antigua, Guatemala.

"Holy shit, Marshall," Joe excitedly repeated.

"I thought I sank your boat again," he exclaimed with animated gestures.

"What happened?" Marshall asked, now concerned as he glanced around.

At first scan, he didn't see anything out of the ordinary. He

looked at the instruments and everything appeared normal—
except for Joe, who was still breathing rapidly.

Joe excitedly continued. "I was sitting here looking out over
the ocean when all of a sudden out of nowhere a white light
came streaking toward the boat at torpedo speed. I glanced
over to the other side and another one was coming at us from
that direction also. I thought we were under attack. My heart
almost jumped out of my chest and all I could do was yell '*Holy
shit.*' I thought I had sunk your boat again until I heard this huge
splash and two porpoises surfaced above the water right next to
the hull. I about had a heart attack on the spot. That light stuff
under the water is really weird. What is it?"

Marshall had to laugh, relieved to know that the emergency
was Joe experiencing his first episode with phosphorescence.

"What is that stuff?" Joe asked again, blushing. "I was sure a
torpedo was sinking us."

Marshall laughingly explained, "A single-celled micro-
scopic alga called *dinoflagellate* caused your torpedo. They're
throughout the ocean and emit light when they are mechani-
cally disturbed by something like a porpoise swimming through
the water." Marshall chuckled again. "This leads to a chemical
reaction within the organism that produces the light show."

Joe, relieved, said, "Hey, sorry about that. Go back to bed.
I'll try to keep things quiet up here the rest of the watch, but
that stuff is weird."

The remainder of the trip with Joe went fairly smoothly, except for a few minor events. He was held in house arrest for one day
in Costa Rica after he discovered he had left his passport at home.
Marshall and I had to take an eight-hour cab ride to the Nicaraguan
border to get a special form that would allow him to enter the
country. But all in all, we could consider the trip to be uneventful
in comparison to our last cruising experience with Joe.

After he left us in Costa Rica, Nicole, our youngest daugh-

ter, joined us for two months while we cruised through Central
America, traversed the Panama Canal, and traveled up the
western Caribbean, stopping along the way to enjoy the many
cultures we passed. In March 1997, four years to the month
after we lost *Clambake*, we arrived in the Bahamas and traveled
down to the Turks, grandmother's birthplace. We had reached
our new goal and destination.

Two weeks after we arrived in the Bahaman chain, we got a
call from Marshall's folks that Nana had died.

At that point we began thinking about the possibility of selling *White Eagle*. We had done a total refit of her in Ensenada; she
was in prime condition. Sailboats were getting a much higher
price on the East Coast than on the West Coast, so even though
we weren't quite ready to sell her, the timing and the market
were perfect. If ever we were going to make the change, now
was the time and Florida was the place.

We still dreamed of Tahiti but believed our ocean-passage
days were over. We had been gone for more than seven years,
and were ready to return to the calm, protected waters of the
Pacific Northwest, where a powerboat would be more practical. Once we sold *White Eagle* we hoped to buy another boat
and travel those beautiful, quiet, inland passages for the rest
of our lives. Perhaps one day we could travel to Tahiti via air. It
wouldn't be quite the same as arriving in our boat, but at this
point in our lives, we figured it would have to do.

Little did we realize we had one more adventure just around
the corner.

CHAPTER 26

The Phone Call

IN MAY 1998 WE BOUGHT PENGUIN ON THE COURTHOUSE steps in Fort Lauderdale. We had been looking at boats for about a month when we stumbled into a repo yard. That was where we spotted the Monk-designed sundeck motor yacht *Jammin*.

The broker told us she was owned by a bank and had been repossessed when the owner had stopped making payments. The boat had been stripped to bare essentials. In addition, she had a large hole in her side and lots of interior dry rot. Former owners had even removed the knobs off the throttles.

After we went over every inch of her, Marshall called to me, "Dee, come here and sit down. Let's talk for a minute. I think we can make this boat work. It's not exactly what I was looking for, but I see potential in her."

"Do you really think she is repairable?"

"I think most of the damage is cosmetic, although I'm concerned that I might be underestimating what it will cost to bring her back. We would need to have the engines checked and make sure there is no problem there. The engines alone could be a $50,000 problem if they need to be replaced."

I thought about what he was saying and then responded, "I like the layout. She would work great for having the family aboard, with the three staterooms. But it sure looks like a lot of work. It's a little overwhelming. And that smell—what on earth is that smell?"

"Oh, I figured that one out. You're going to love this. The holding tank has overflowed into the bilge."

"Great. That should be a lot of fun to clean up," I chided.

I thought about what Marshall had said a few minutes more.

"You know, I think this could be a good boat for us. But I agree, we would have to buy her right. I think these repairs could really add up."

The more time we spent on her, the more we grew to like her and the more excited we became about bidding at the auction.

The following day Marshall told me, "I've done some calculating on what would need to be done to bring her back, and as long as we keep our bid in the $100,000-range, I think we will be okay and can't get hurt—that is, so long as the engines check out. I'll try to find someone to come out today who can do an oil analysis on the transmission and main engine. I talked to the broker, and because the boat is still impounded, that's about all they will allow us to do."

"Sounds reasonable, but the salesman said the owner still owed the bank more than $180,000. Do you think the bank would go that low?"

"Banks aren't in the business of owning boats. You never know how much of a loss they are willing to absorb."

"It sure seems like there has been a lot of interest in her. Every time we go out to the repo yard, someone else is always there looking, too."

"I know. That concerns me. I wish we had some idea what the bids are. The broker said he already had three."

"Maybe if we talk to him, he can give us a suggestion where to begin our bidding. What do ya' think?"

"I'm sure they can't give out any information. We'll just have to make our sealed bid based on what she is worth to us and hope for the best."

Later that day, after Marshall was satisfied with the oil analysis, we submitted a sealed bid of $113,000 just before the deadline.

The bids were opened on a Wednesday afternoon. It was about four o'clock before we stopped by the yard to find out the results. We were high bidder. When the broker told us the good news, I almost reached out to give him a big kiss, I was so excited. Instead. I kissed Marshall.

"Oh, my God, Marshall, we got the boat. Boy, will we have our work cut out for us over the next couple of years."

Marshall was excited, too, but right now his mind was occupied with the million and one things he would need to do to her before we could take her back home through the canal.

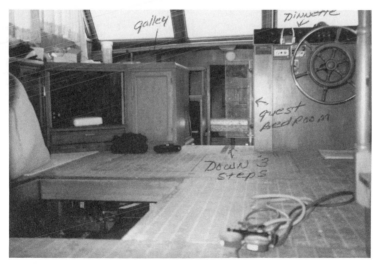

Penguin's condition at the time of auction. We had a dream . . .

We signed the paperwork that the broker had prepared and gave him a $10,000 deposit. It was going to be a couple of days before the boat could be released to us. We were told the final paperwork would have to be court approved.

After a week, with the salesman still making excuses why we couldn't take possession of our new purchase, we became quite concerned. Frustrated, we finally contacted the sheriff's office that was handling the foreclosure. The clerk put us in touch with the judge who was handling the case.

Then we found out why the delay. The sale at the repo yard had been illegal. The official foreclosure sale had not yet occurred. The boat brokers had gotten overzealous when they saw all the activity the boat had created and had held the auction prematurely and illegally. We didn't own the boat.

We confronted the broker; he sheepishly admitted his error and refunded our deposit.

"Now what do we do, Marshall?" I asked disappointedly.

"I don't see why we can't attend the court auction on our own."

"There still appears to be a lot of interest in the boat. I wonder how many others are thinking of attending the auction?"

We tracked down the attorney who represented the bank and talked to him several times on the phone. Because he represented the bank, the information we were able to obtain from him was limited, but he confirmed that there was a fair amount of interest and possibly as many as three or four others might be bidding. We had to decide how high we were willing to bid.

The bank already was aware of our offer of $113,000 so we assumed the opening bid would begin there. We didn't want to get caught up in the moment of the bidding, so we decided we would only go as high as $130,000 and then walk away. If it didn't work, there would always be another boat.

You can imagine our surprise when we showed up on the courthouse steps on the day of the sale and found only one other gentleman there. He turned out to be the attorney representing the bank, the one we had talked with several times on the phone.

The clerk from the sheriff's office arrived at the exact advertised time. She announced the auction.

"Hear ye, hear ye, all those interested in the sale of the motor vessel *Jammin* please come forward."

She asked us to sign the register and then turned to the attorney and asked, "At what price does the bank wish to open the bidding?"

We were prepared for the auction to begin at $113.000 dollars, my mouth dropped open in shock when he responded, "$50,000."

The clerk asked, "Are there any other bids?"

My mouth dropped open even wider when Marshall responded, "I bid $75,000."

I had expected him to go right to our former bid of $113,000. The attorney was on the cell phone with the bank. We heard him tell someone, "They just offered $75,000; what do you want me to do?"

Meanwhile, the clerk hit her gavel on the podium and said, "Going once."

The attorney repeated the question into the cell phone, "What do you want me to do?"

"Going twice." The clerk banged her gavel again.

We watched the expression on the face of the attorney go blank as he listened to someone on the other end of the phone, and we turned just in time to see the clerk bang down her gavel for the third time.

"Going three times. Sold to the Saunders for $75,000."

Marshall and I looked at each other with mouths agape.

What had just happened? We knew there was a loan against the boat for $183,000 still owed to the bank by the original owner. We expected the bank to eat some of the loan, but why did they let it go so low? The attorney seemed baffled, too.

We followed the clerk to her office and signed the necessary papers. She explained that there would be a three-day waiting period and the judge would have to sign the final papers granting the sale legal.

Those were the longest three days. We knew this was too good to be true and something would go wrong. The attorney assured us the bank couldn't do anything to retract the sale, because he was there to represent it. Each day we called the sheriff's office to see if there were any rebuttals.

Three days came and went, the judge approved the sale, and *Jammin* was ours.

The first thing we did was change her name to *Penguin*. It seemed to fit us. She was slow and wallowed. We traveled slow and waddled. Penguins loved the water and didn't like to fly—just like us. Penguins also mated for life. The name seemed to fit just right.

She was quite a sight, which translated to about a year's worth of work to make her cruise-ready, safe, and comfortable. But it was worth the wait and the work. She was perfect for us.

While in Florida we heard about United Yacht Transport, the super float-a-boat/freighter that transports yachts around the world while owners ride with their yachts. We checked with its main office in Fort Lauderdale and found that they had a freighter scheduled to leave in a couple of weeks. That would barely provide enough time for Marshall to patch the hole in the hull, buy some basic electronics, and make a few other minor repairs that would be essential before leaving. But the timing was perfect, and we were getting eager to get her to the Pacific Northwest. The freighter's itinerary took us through the Panama Canal to the west coast of Mexico. This would save a lot of time and take the pressure off getting all the repairs done before we left Florida. We signed up to ride piggyback.

We hoped to spend about six months on Mexico's west coast to make repairs and wait for the hurricane season to pass. We then planned to head up the coast on *Penguin*'s own bottom and ultimately arrive in the Pacific Northwest.

Less than two months after purchasing *Penguin* on the courthouse steps in Fort Lauderdale, we arrived in Lazaro Cardenas, a Mexican west-coast port city known for its steel industry. We quickly traveled up the coast to picturesque Bahía De Navidad, a fairly safe haven during hurricanes, where a 400-foot-high, triangular-faced pyramid, the largest of the islands, and rocks extending southward from the coast, protected the resort/marina of Barra de Navidad. We would spend several months there restoring and repairing our new home.

Those months passed quickly and *Penguin* was close to being cruise-ready. We had been working diligently on the inside problems. Now it was time to turn our attention to her exterior. Marshall had just gotten an estimate to have the boat painted when we heard on the ham radio that the transport/freighter was returning to Mexico. Marshall called the company to see if by chance they had a route scheduled to travel north to Vancouver, B.C. Instead he was given information on a leg traveling to the South Pacific.

He turned tome after hanging up the phone. "That was an interesting conversation with the transport's main office."

"What did you find out?" I asked.

"They have another leg leaving in two weeks that could drop us off in Tahiti and six months later pick us up and take us to Vancouver. They still have space available and the company is willing to give us a deal. It would cost us about the same as having the boat painted. What do you think—heads, we go to Tahiti; tails, we paint the boat."

I smiled at the thought. We had been given a second chance at life when the Korean freighter rescued us; now we were given a second chance to achieve our Tahitian dream.

My answer was obvious. "Don't even bother to flip the coin. I can live with a chalky-white hull."

One more adventure lay ahead of us.

CHAPTER 27

Can Fate Intervene Again?

THREE WEEKS LATER, AROUND THE MIDDLE OF FEBRUARY 1999, Marshall and I loaded *Penguin* onto the *Super Servant IV* Transport. After years of planning, Marshall's phone call had opened the door to our dream. At long last we found ourselves again on the way to Tahiti. The weather was calm and the initial days on the freighter dragged by, reminding me how slowly time can appear to pass. My mind frequently drifted back to the night, five years earlier, when we first made this same ocean passage. That night, time also seemed to stand still.

My muscles tightened as I visualized us once again perched on our upside-down Zodiac, straining our eyes for any sign that the huge freighter that just ran us down was turning back to rescue us. My breathing became more rapid as I envisioned the distant lights of the huge ship disappearing slowly over the black horizon into the night. A shiver shot down my spine and a feeling of uneasiness crept over me. Part of the apprehension, I reasoned, stemmed from envisioning the nightmare of that horrible night, but part of it was just an ominous feeling.

Looking from the bow of Penguin *after other boats have been loaded on the* Super Servant IV.

Even though the first week aboard the freighter went by uneventfully allowing us time to paint *Penguin's* bottom, replace the zincs, and get a lot of other minor work done, I continued to feel apprehensive

For several days, our captain, a tall, good-looking Danish gentleman, had been tracking a hurricane that was barreling north and that eventually *could* intercept our path if the timing was right. I worried that fate again would interfere and somehow prevent us from reaching our dream.

That night I tossed and turned as mental images darted in and out of my nightmare of all the possible catastrophes that could happen. During waking moments, I could feel the huge ship rolling as the seas and the winds continued to build. I knew the hurricane was approaching. I wondered how safe we were, strapped in our cradle riding piggyback in the so-called protection of the huge transport.

At dinner on the 13th day, the day before we were to make landfall, our captain announced that the harbormaster at Papeete had closed the port to all ships entering or leaving. Huge waves reportedly were breaking across the entrance. Again, I couldn't stop wondering if something could go wrong.

I expressed my concerns to Marshall.

"Don't worry, we're safe on this freighter," he confidently assured me. "Besides, you're with me, and I have the Colgate shield around me."

I looked up at him with one of my *yeah, right* expressions

"Trust me, it will be okay." He grinned one of his infectious grins. "We're going to make it to Tahiti."

Why did I feel so apprehensive?

It was with great anxiety that I crawled into bed that evening and finally drifted off to sleep. When Marshall nudged me awake the following morning, I sighed my relief.

I mumbled sleepily, "Today we should hopefully reach landfall."

Marshall smiled at me. "You really are worried, aren't you? See, I told you we would be okay. No mishaps last night, no meeting with the hurricane," he chided.

Again I sighed and thought, *life is good. Fate has not intervened yet.*

We had our normal breakfast with the crew and hurriedly joined the rest of the yacht owners who were gathering on the bridge to watch for landfall.

It was day 14. The sky was black and ominous. The seas were horrendous. Winds were blowing a steady 45 knots with gusts much stronger. The captain had slowed the freighter to try to avoid the hurricane and to make the ride more comfortable. We were taking 10-degree rolls, and the spray was coming up over the bridge. The massive waves were frightening and mesmerizing.

As we strained our eyes for the first sight of land, I heard one of the other owners comment, "Boy, am I glad I'm riding piggyback on the transport this trip instead of out there on my own boat."

We all nodded and agreed.

Finally, I thought I saw something in the distance. At about the same moment, one of the other yacht owners yelled, "There's land."

I pointed into the distance and nearly jumped for joy. "Marshall, I think I see it on the horizon. There it is . . . yes, there's Tahiti."

As I looked out at distant, barely visible palm trees, I remembered our conversation the day we sat on the shores of Lake Eagle planning our future twenty years ago. This was not how we had envisioned our arrival in Tahiti, but it did not diminish the magic of the moment. The combination of seeing landfall, which is every sailor's ultimate climax of a voyage, plus the thought of finally achieving our goal, generated an incredible high, and a union between us that could not be put in words.

Marshall put his arm around me and pulled me close, sharing the moment.

As I stood watching the twinkle return to Marshall's eyes, the twinkle that I hadn't seen much of since *Clambake* had sunk almost five years ago, a flood of emotion enveloped me. I felt blessed to be sharing this adventure with such a wonderful man. It was at this moment that I realized we were here because of Marshall's incredible unfailing talents and knowledge, and the determination and belief in myself given to me by my mother. The echo of her words always was a constant reminder that "You can do it." And it appeared we just did.

In a few short hours we would arrive at the island of our dreams. For years our focus had been to traverse the ocean and spend blissful days cruising the South Pacific Islands. Now that land finally was in sight and our dream within reach, the thought again crossed my mind, *Could fate intervene one more time?* Even riding piggyback in the security of the huge freighter and so close to the harbor, I couldn't stop wondering if somehow destiny would keep us from reaching our goal.

The harbor finally came into view. The swells were enormous. Some of the waves were breaking across the entrance into frothy explosions. The captain brought the huge transport around slowly and began lining her up on the markers. I knew the waves were large enough to make the narrow entrance dangerous even for a huge ship. There was no room for the slightest error, for the reef could be deadly.

All of the yacht owners and their captains were on the bridge watching the maneuver with macabre fascination. I gripped Marshall's arm; my body tensed as we continued to close on the pass. The ship was heading toward the entrance in line with the range markers. The wind was gusting from the beam and pushed the freighter sideways.

The mood on the bridge suddenly changed from excitement to solemn concern. No one moved, no one spoke as we watched the massive ship close on the entrance. We could see that the freighter was being shoved sideways and was no longer in the perfect position to enter.

My heart beat rapidly.

Finally, Marshall broke the silence. "He best be turning out, or it looks to me like we're going to be on the reef."

Everyone remained silent. Tenseness and apprehension hung in the air.

Just before the point of no return, the captain turned the ship hard to starboard and broke off to try another approach. With my arm still linked through Marshall's, I exhaled a sigh of relief as the captain slowly turned the freighter back into deeper water and initiated his approach one more time. This time he came in at a slightly different angle to allow room for the gusts to push the ship sideways.

The second attempt ended as did the first. Once again, we watched in silence as he turned the freighter out into deeper water. This time, our captain announced over the speakers that he would try one more run. If this didn't work, we would stand off the entrance until conditions improved.

It took the captain 40 minutes to realign the ship for his last try at the pass. Once again he lined up the freighter on the entrance range markers. He approached slowly and cautiously, again ready to veer off to starboard if necessary. He was timing the waves.

Clinging to Marshall and with my voice close to a quaver, I asked, "Do you think he will make it this time?"

He paused for a moment, surveying the situation before answering. "I think the angle is a lot better this approach. I think he can make it if he maintains his speed."

Within a few seconds we shot through the narrow entrance and into the protective harbor waters. Sighs of relief and applause of joy broke out among the yacht owners.

Ahead of us lay the palm-lined quay with the boats med-tied in a line. There didn't appear to be much room for a freighter full of more yachts. But our thoughts turned to absorb all the sights and sounds of this bustling island city and to watch the freighter docking at its own designated space right in the center of the harbor.

"Oh, Marshall, it's even more picturesque than I imagined," I murmured as I tried to take in the beauty and activity at the same time.

With his arm around my waist, he smiled and squeezed me tightly. He didn't need to say anything. I could tell by the look in his eyes how pleased he was that I was already enjoying the beauty and enchantment of the islands.

The docking went smoothly, as did the unloading of the yachts, and before we realized it we were snug in our slip at the marina just a few miles from the bustling city.

We had made it safely to Tahiti. Our adventures in the Society Islands were about to begin.

CHAPTER 28

Tahiti

REMINISCING ABOUT THE SIX MONTHS WE SPENT IN THE South Pacific, I visualize storybook settings: Tropical palm trees with thatched roof huts against a backdrop of majestic purple volcanic peaks, beautiful young topless Tahitian girls with flowers in their long black hair paddling by our boat in dug-out canoes, crystal-clear sparkling blue waters in hues that a camera can't do justice to, deserted stretches of white sand beaches, and fishermen in their brightly painted *pangas* with the catch of the day buzzing around the harbors. It truly was the paradise we had dreamed about for years, with its addicting, unhurried way of life.

It is easy for me to understand why three young surfers from California bought land and settled in Moorea in the early '50s, ultimately building the famous Bali Hai Hotel on the beach. It was idyllic. The lagoon in front of their hotel turned out to be one of our favorite anchorages, and the hotel a favorite haunt. I still can close my eyes and clearly envision Marshall and me lazily lounging on *Penguin's* back sundeck in front of the Bali Hai, gazing idly at the incredible lush tropical flora surrounding the thatched roof bungalows of their resort, with the whole setting backdropped by the majestic distant jagged peaks of Mt. Rotui.

Marshall relaxes aboard Penguin *in front of the Bali Hai, Morea.*

The view was dramatic and breathtaking. It always amazed us that most of the other sailboats clustered in the larger Cook's Bay around the corner when this was such an incredible idyllic anchorage. We usually had it all to ourselves.

However, all was not perfect in Paradise. By the end of the first week, I thought we had made a grave mistake in committing ourselves to six months in these islands. After the initial paperwork with the French bureaucracy, the majority of other boats that traveled with us on the transport scattered off to distant destinations. The Americas Cup was scheduled for later that year, and many of the larger yachts were on their way to Australia to be part of the festivities. We were stranded. There was no escape. Our travel was limited to the island chain in which we had been deposited. Once arriving there via freighter, there was no way we could leave on *Penguin's* bottom until the freighter returned to pick us up six month later. *Penguin* did not have the fuel capacity to cross the 3,000-mile stretch home. Although she is a great coastal cruiser, she was not designed for an ocean crossing.

In addition, after our new freighter friends left, we appeared to be the only Americans cruising in the area. All of our encounters with other cruisers seemed to be with people who spoke only French. The first couple of weeks we found ourselves exploring more for other people who spoke English than we did to see the local sights.

In hindsight, I think we would have enjoyed that first month a lot more if we had taken the time before our arrival to learn French so we could communicate more with the locals. It wasn't that we didn't try to socialize with other boaters; our efforts always ended in shrugs of indifference. We had the distinct feeling *they* did not want to make the effort to communicate with us.

I can vividly remember sitting across from Marshall in the cockpit after coming back from one of our daily excursions and remarking, "This may be a long six months."

"I was just thinking that exact same thing," was his solemn reply.

"When do you think the first sailboats making the milk run from Mexico across to Tahiti will start arriving?" I asked.

"Well, let me think about that. The earliest they would leave Mexico is usually mid-March. They should arrive in the Marqueses two to three weeks later; then they probably will stop off in the Tuamotus for a couple of weeks, so the first boats could be arriving here the second to third week in April."

"Wow. That's six weeks away. That's a long time not to speak English to anyone. It sure would be helpful to know a little more than our 20 words in French." I sighed in frustration and went back to studying my French-English dictionary.

"It seems they just don't want to associate with us. Maybe

it's because we are power boaters and everyone else is a sail-
boater. What do you think it is?' I asked Marshall

"I don't know, Dee. I remember the last time I was here
with Missy and Tiffany it was the same way. The French were
distant to us and the Tahitians were incredibly friendly, even
though we didn't speak either language."

"How did you and Missy handle the situation?" I asked.

"We just did our own thing—exploring, snorkeling—and
the time seemed to fly by."

"I guess that's what we need to do, then. Besides, it's only a
few weeks until our first set of company arrives. We need to get
to know the area so we can show them a good time."

As Marshall predicted, about the middle of April the first
sailboats crossing the Pacific started to arrive, and it wasn't long
before we developed some new friendships amongst the cruising fleet. After that, time did fly by.

In the interim, after tiring of city life in Papeete, we decided to explore the more remote Leeward Islands: Moorea,
Huahine, Raiatea, and Bora Bora. We determined it was pru-
dent to start with Moorea, the closest.

We soon discovered that crossings between the islands and
entering the passes through the reefs could be a real challenge.
The large Pacific Ocean swells seemed to be present virtually
all of the time; the wave action often pushed us toward the reef
without our being aware of it. Also, winds consistently funneled
through the channels, creating seas that had 3,000-plus miles to
build. The swells appeared to come from every direction, gen-
erating a cabbage-patch or washing-machine condition—very
uncomfortable, especially since *Penguin* was not equipped with
stabilizers.

On one crossing between Huahine and Moorea, we had to
duck back through a pass into a protected lagoon shortly after we
left the anchorage. As we left the sheltered waters of the harbor,

Marshall remarked, "This should be a good trip. The ocean appears to be at rest and conditions look perfect for traveling."

I agreed that they did.

However, as we passed around the end of the island, we ran into horrendous seas that appeared to be building. The waves were coming up over the second-story fly bridge, and the troughs were too steep to turn *Penguin* around safely. Marshall turned her bow into the seas and continued around the tip to a point far enough past the end of the island so that when he made the turn, we would not be caught in the trough.

"Check the charts and see if you can find any place for us to tuck back in behind the reef safely," he calmly ordered.

I scanned our charts and found, just a short distance ahead, a break in the reef that appeared to be safe to wait out the weather. We continued until we spotted the opening. We knew we needed to stay well out from the barrier reef before attempting to enter the pass.

"Hold on," he ordered. "I'm going to bring her around and try to turn in. This could be nasty."

Penguin took a sharp roll as Marshall kicked the starboard engine in reverse, keeping the port engine in forward turning a hard 90 degrees. He navigated her safely through the opening in the reef before another wave was able to catch us broadside.

We soon found ourselves in an isolated lagoon, a tropical paradise filled with fragrant flowers, coconut palm groves, and exotic birds. There was no sign of other humans living in the area. This was exactly how I envisioned the deserted islands of the South Pacific. We were beginning to feel like Robinson Crusoe.

Three days later the seas calmed down, enabling us, with some regrets, to leave this little bit of unspoiled paradise. We made the passage back to Moorea without a problem.

After we got past looking for local camaraderie, we fell

into a routine similar to our cruising days in Mexico: Exploring, snorkeling, fishing, and just relaxing on our sundeck taking in the incredible beauty surrounding us.

As we had in Mexico, we spent hours in the water enjoying the snorkeling. It's hard to put into words the unbelievable splendor under the sea in the Society Islands. Marshall often had described to me the gigantic fan coral that he had seen so much of 15 years earlier. He was eager to share that beauty with me, but he was disappointed when we were unable to find much of it remaining. We searched all of his favorite snorkeling haunts but couldn't find any of the fan coral that he remembered being so prolific. Although we saw lots of other types of coral and tropical fish, our search for the elusive fan coral ended in vain.

We questioned the locals, "What happened to all the fan coral?"

Most of them didn't have any good explanation, but blamed their disappearance on everything from severe hurricanes to boaters dropping their anchors on the coral and destroying it, and, of course, to pollution.

We later read a magazine article in which a marine biologist theorized that the disappearance of the coral stemmed from severely elevated water temperatures caused by El Niño. He felt it was the single most important stress event experienced by these corals over the past three centuries. A process he referred to as *bleaching*, occurs when the coral animal comes under any kind of life-threatening stress, and the host polyp evicts its algae. Without its symbiotic partner, corals can live only a month or so before they die.

One of the highlights of our snorkeling adventures was our encounter with stingrays. Daily we watched tour boats zoom by our anchorage and head to the far side of the island. One day we decided to follow in our Zodiac and watch where and how they fed the stingrays. We soon learned their schedules and became

Dee and Marshall Saunders. (photo courtesy Sidonia StGermaine)

a guide service for our own guests, being careful not to overlap with the scheduled tour groups.

The rays were huge, soft to the touch and incredibly friendly and curious. They would eat small pieces of fish out of our hands as they let us stroke their velvety skin. We never tired, nor did our friends or family, of surrounding ourselves with these wonderful sea creatures.

In Bora Bora we created our own E ride, equating to the most exciting ride at Disneyland. There was one particular spot not far from Bloody Mary's restaurant where the current passed rapidly through a narrow opening in the reef. We would take our dinghy to the far end of that reef, hop overboard garbed with fins and snorkel, and then, each grabbing a rope attached to the dinghy, ride the current to the opposite end. These fast-moving currents attracted a lot of the larger fish, including the ubiquitous sharks, huge barracudas, and majestic manta rays. Some, such as the six-foot-long trumpet fish, were just curious. They would come close to us and hang motionless, just observing. Other fish lingered in the distance, just barely a flickering shadow against the deep canyons of the coral below. For the most part, larger fish ignored us, but I felt much safer knowing I was attached to our dinghy if I needed to make a quick exit to safety.

During the six months spent in these beautiful islands, we anchored out all but about two weeks—the week we arrived and the week we left. In most cases we had no choice, for the marinas were expensive and few and far between. But we enjoyed being on anchor and found that the only negative aspect was the frequent squalls. The weather would change from beautiful and calm to winds that gusted to 60 knots within what seemed like minutes. Half of the time we were anchored in only seven or eight feet of water, with coral reefs close by, and the rest we were in waters nearly 100 feet deep. Either way, when a squall passed over we spent many harrowing moments hoping our anchor would hold.

The good thing was that as quickly as the squalls had arrived, they were gone. The day would return to extraordinary beauty and calm, leaving only multiple brilliant rainbows as a reminder of what had just passed our way.

Weeks slipped by as we found many new secluded beaches and coves to explore, made many new friendships, and saw family and friends come and go. Before we realized it, the six months had skated by. The freighter was to return and pick us up at the end of August. It was time to head back to Papeete to prepare for our journey back to Vancouver.

CHAPTER 29

The End and the Beginning

THE SHIP ARRIVED ON SCHEDULE AND THE BOARDING OF 14 yachts went smoothly. Our departure from Papeete was completely opposite our arrival. The seas were calm and the day was beautiful, making it all the more difficult to say our goodbyes.

In contrast to most of the yacht owners aboard the freighter who were starting a new adventure, we were seeing the culmination of ours. Marshall and I stood on the wing deck alone, watching the palm trees of Tahiti fade in the distance. It was a somber moment. Neither of us had much to say.

I knew Marshall was riding the same emotional roller coaster I was. Tahiti had been our dream, our goal for so many years. It was difficult to put into perspective that we achieved it, we lived it . . . and now it was over. We had been so busy enjoying the six months in Paradise that the thought never crossed our minds that it would end, and with it our dream. We had never talked about what we would do *after* Tahiti.

As the palm trees faded from sight, Marshall and I slowly meandered back to *Penguin*. She was safely nestled in her cradle welded to the steel deck of the freighter, and as we passed by her bottom, we saw again that she was much in need of some maintenance. We climbed the ladder to her back deck and stopped to rest and discuss which project to begin first. We made a plan and set off to get some work done that very day.

The captain predicted the trip to Vancouver would be calm so we were hoping to get a lot of maintenance completed before we reached port. The seas were tranquil and it made moving around the cradles no more difficult than doing the job on land.

Days again clicked by. We had finished the necessary work on *Penguin* and took to reading and visiting with other yacht owners to pass the days.

One afternoon while sitting on our back deck reading, I paused to look up at Marshall. The twinkle in his eye was becoming elusive. I studied him as he sat there with his book perched on his knee. I finally burst out, "We need to set some new goals."

"Fine," he uttered indifferently. "What goals do you want to set?"

"I don't know," I answered despondently. "But I feel we need something to look forward to when we get back home." I paused for a moment and then asked, "If you could do anything, what would you want to do?"

"I don't know. I haven't thought much about it."

I wanted to continue this conversation, but I could tell this discussion wasn't going to go anywhere. I dropped the subject and switched to asking Marshall, "Where do you think we should keep *Penguin* when we get back to Vancouver?"

"My thought was to spend a little time at several marinas as we travel down the coast toward Anacortes," he answered. "I'm sure a lot has changed over the nine years we have been gone.

We can see who has space available and then decide which one would work best."

"Sounds like a plan," I agreed.

The conversation ended and we returned to reading. I decided not to bring up goal planning for the remainder of the trip. Marshall's mood was not conducive to making plans for the future right now, and being truthful with myself, neither was mine. Leaving Tahiti had been like falling down the backside of one huge crest of a wave; it was going to take time to crawl back out of the trough.

After passing through the Straits of Juan De Fuca and nearing Vancouver, the yacht owners gathered on the bridge to watch for the first sign of lights of the big city. Eyes were peeled on the horizon, and you could tell by the chatter that the others were eager to begin their new adventure. However, for Marshall and me it was different. It was with combined emotions of excitement and sadness that we stood silently together, watching for the distant lights. I was eager to be back close to our family but sad to see our nine years of cruising far-away lands come to a culmination. Marshall's silence told me he also was sad to see our trip end.

For the first time in months, there was a definite coolness in the air and I pulled a sweater around my shoulders. Marshall put his arm around me and pulled me close. Then I saw the first glow of lights in the distance. At the same moment, it was like a light suddenly turned on inside my mind.

I had been thinking a lot about what we could do when we got back to the Pacific Northwest. Although I hadn't brought the subject up again with Marshall, the fact that we didn't have a plan was bothering me, and I kept mulling possibilities over in my mind. Then it hit me.

Of course, I thought. *I was too busy riding out the last crest of the wave not to realize it before. We don't need a new goal right now. Just as a door opened for us when Marshall made the call to the transport company in Mexico giving us the opportunity to achieve our dream, there will be other doors giving us other opportunities.*

As the lights of Vancouver became clearer on the horizon, so did our future. I nearly jumped for joy.

"Marshall, do you know what has just become unmistakably apparent to me? We don't *need* a new goal or plan."

"What are you talking about?" He looked at me as if I had just lost my mind.

I relayed to him what I had just discovered. My thoughts flowed freely, the words tumbling out of my mouth as I reminisced about our past together and explored our unknown future. He listened with interest.

I rambled on about how destiny had thrown us many challenges and we met them all. Our life had been sunk beneath us when Tiffany died, but we were spurred on with a new appreciation for life itself. When fate took *Clambake* and our dream of Tahiti to the ocean's bottom, we persevered and pressed forward with new determination. We hurdled each of the challenges that destiny had cast us and finally, together, had reached our goal. We had reached Tahiti. Paradise was found. That part of our journey was complete.

I paused for a moment smiling as I looked up into his eyes. "I guess what I am trying to say is that Tahiti was just a kick-start for the future. I know we want a lot more out of life. I also know that a new adventure is just one day or one telephone call away." I shrugged my shoulders and grinned. "Who knows what new adventure or challenge fate will throw our way tomorrow?"

Marshall smiled and I saw the twinkle return in his eyes.

At that moment I knew we were going to be okay. As my mother's words once again echoed in my mind, "You can do it," I realized that no matter what fate threw our way, we would survive. I *now* knew that together, we could not be sunk forever.

AFTER STORY

AFTER THE FREIGHTER DELIVERED US TO VANCOUVER, WE made our new home at Roche Harbor in Washington's San Juan Islands. Within a year, Marshall and I were diagnosed with cancer. We went through treatment together, each giving support to the other. Once again, while sitting in the waiting room awaiting our treatments, we were reminded of how short and fragile life is as we witnessed so many others so close to the end. We were grateful we had retired when we did and that we had nine wonderful years of cruising together.

Two years later, both cancer-free, we bought a home on Whidbey Island, and now are cruising the inside passages back and forth to Alaska every summer and sharing the joys of boating with our family, children, grandchildren, and friends. We keep a wide berth from all freighters.

But I still feel a slight twinge every time I see the name Hanjin on a freighter or passing truck.

ABOUT THE AUTHOR

Dee Saunders was born and raised in eastern Pennsylvania and attended East Stroudsburg State College. She moved to San Jose, California in the early 1960s and married. She later became a real estate agent and moved to Northern California. Soon after the move, the marriage dissolved.

Marshall Saunders lived on a sailboat with his wife and daughter in Honolulu, where he owned several dental laboratories. In the late 1970s, his marriage dissolved and he moved to Northern California where he changed professions and became a real estate broker. It was in northern California where Dee and Marshall ultimately met, married, and joined families.

Together they opened a Real Estate brokerage in the small mountain community of Shingletown and lived there until retiring in their mid-forties to the cruising lifestyle. Marshall had been sailing all his life, but Dee was new to the adventures. Early in the relationship they did a lot of racing on various sailboats including the Hobie 18, Stelleto 27 and Olson 25. After retiring, they spent nine years living aboard their Tayana 52 and later after their accident, their Tatoosh 51 cruising the waters of British Columbia, Alaska, Mexico, Central and South America, the western Caribbean, the Bahamas and the South Pacific putting many miles of open ocean cruising under their belt.

Dee and her husband, Marshall, currently reside on Whidbey Island and own a Newberry Port 52 sundeck trawler, on which they spend their summers cruising to Northern British Columbia and Alaska.